Management Ideas

. . . in brief

3/71

This book is dedicated to:

■ My wife Laura and my children Jenny, Susan and Peter.

■ To all those business executives/employees who have gone through and are going through the traumas and perhaps pleasures of change and those who have become casualties of organizational transformation.

■ All my colleagues at the Economist Conferences.

Management Ideas
...in brief

Sultan Kermally

Butterworth-Heinemann
Linacre House, Jordan Hill, Oxford OX2 8DP
A division of Reed Educational and Professional Publishing Ltd

ℛ A member of the Reed Elsevier plc group

OXFORD   BOSTON   JOHANNESBURG
MELBOURNE   NEW DELHI   SINGAPORE

First published 1997

British Library Cataloguing in Publication Data
A catalogue record for this book is available from the British
Library

ISBN 0 7506 3450 2

Composition by Scribe Design, Gillingham, Kent
Printed and bound in Great Britain by
Biddles Ltd, Guildford and King's Lynn

Contents

Acknowledgements

This book would have not been possible without the help of individuals and the organizations and publishers who have given me permission to reproduce conference presentations, extracts from the journals and the books. My thanks go to:

All my students and those executives with whom I have come into contact at training sessions and conferences who planted the idea for this book.

- Henri Aebischer of Apple Computer Europe.
- David Allen-Butler, Business Operations Manager, Digital Systems, Digital Equipment Co.
- American Management Association, USA.
- Anglo-German Foundation for the Study of Industrial Society, London. (Extract from the report, Managing in Britain and Germany.)
- BBC Worldwide Ltd.
- Martin Brackenbury, Thomson Travel Group.
- *Business Week*: Benchmarking at Work: Improving procurement (Dec 1993).
- Nick Butcher, Managing Director, DHL Int (UK) Ltd.
- Butterworth–Heinemann, Oxford, UK.
- Department of Trade and Industry, UK.
- Digital Equipment Co., Reading, UK.
- European Foundation for Quality Management, Avenue des Pleiades 19, 1200 Brussels.
- Harvard Business School Publishing, How to Make Reengineering Really Work. (Nov–Dec, 1995). Gene Hall, Jim Rosenthal, Judy Wade. Putting the Balanced Score-card to Work (Sept–Oct, 1993). Robert Kaplan and David P. Norton.
- Richard Haydon, Artemis International, Slough, UK.
- International Institute for Management Development, Lausanne, Switzerland.
- Sune Karlsson, Customer-Focus Coordinator, ABB, Manheim, Germany.

Acknowledgements

- John Kelly, managing director, European Quality Publications Ltd, London. (Extracts published by kind permission, © 1995 European Quality Publications Ltd/UK Publications Ltd.)
- Lloyd's Register Quality Assurance Ltd, Croydon, UK.
- McGraw-Hill Inc. (Extract from *Quality Without Tears*, by P. Crosby.)
- 3M United Kingdom plc. (Conference presentation 'The Lateral Alternatives' by Paul M. Davies, Manager, HRD, Europe.)
- Prentice-Hall Inc. For permission to produce a diagram from page 297 of the book *Principles of Marketing* by Philip Kotler.
- Gareth Rees, chief executive officer, Kinsley Lord Ltd, London.
- Royal Mail, UK.
- The Economist Conferences, 15 Regent Street, London, UK.
- The Economist Intelligence Unit, UK.
- The Times Newspaper, London.
- The Open University Business School, Milton Keynes, UK. (Material from Course B889: Performance Measurement and Evaluation.)
- The McKinsey Quarterly, UK. Reprinted by special permission from Frank Ostroff and Douglas Smith. The Horizontal Organisation. *The McKinsey Quarterly*, 1992. No. 1 © 1992. McKinsey & Co. All rights reserved.
- Graham Witney, partner, Coopers & Lybrand, London.

I am particularly indebted to Jacquie Shanahan from Butterworth–Heinemann for her encouragement and direction and for giving me the opportunity to write this book. My thanks also go to other staff at Butterworth–Heinemann involved in producing this book.

Finally my thanks and affection go to my wife Laura for her support and encouragement and for letting me hide in my study to write this book and my children Jenny, Susan and Peter for their encouragement and enthusiasm.

Sultan Kermally

Introduction

in brief "Management has always been beset by fads and fashions, gurus and demagogues. But never before has there been such a sheer volume of new approaches."
Professor Edward Lawler of the University of Southern California School of Business Administration

Management ideas . . . in brief

This book is about practising total management thinking. It explores key management thinking and ideas of our time and examines how some organizations have taken these ideas on board and incorporated them in their strategies in order to survive in today's intensively competitive climate.

Why this book?

This book is an abridged version of the book *Total Management Thinking* published by Butterworth–Heinemann in

Introduction

1996. The themes and the management issues have remained the same but most of the presentations have been edited or deleted in order to present a compact book on management thinking and practice for those readers whose demands and time constraints are different. I have been involved in management development and training for a number of years. I have a passion for new management thinking and its applicability in the business world in which we live and work.

In my present job as senior vice president and director of the Economist Conferences and in my previous job as senior group director at Management Centre Europe, Brussels, I have come across thousands of business executives who have attended leading edge management conferences and training programmes. The topics of conversation always boil down to the following key aspects of business:

- We cannot cope with the various management fads and thinking that are proliferating in the business world.
- One needs to spend a lot of money and read at least fifteen to twenty books and numerous articles to keep track of what is happening.
- As it is, it is difficult to manage our time. The problem is accentuated by working with less people due to restructuring and downsizing.
- Do these management ideas work in practice and what types of organizations have applied them?
- Wouldn't be nice to have all these issues addressed in one book?

Similar views have been expressed by my MBA students over the years.

As we live in a customer-focused world, I have decided to take these issues on board and meet the demands of customers. I have used presentations made at the Economist Conferences, articles published in professional journals and management reviews, and tried to present the topics in a simple and pragmatic way.

I have also addressed the various concerns and issues raised by the casualties of corporate restructuring and those employees who work in a new environment.

How have the topics been chosen?

All businesses operate within the external environment consisting of sociological, technological, economic and political factors (the **competitive environment**). To respond to these external as well as internal environments, organizations have embarked upon improving the quality of products, processes and people (**total quality management**). To become a quality-driven organization, efforts have to be made to adopt best practice (**benchmarking**). The focus of being the best in class is to deliver service excellence (**customer focus**) and continually to monitor performance in order to sustain best practice (**performance management**).

The race has developed to abandon the status quo and adopt radical thinking in order to eliminate non-value adding activities and be responsive to customer needs (**business process re-engineering**). In such an environment workers have to be given power to solve problems and make decisions (**empowerment**). Streamlining structure due to re-engineering has led to flat organizations (the **horizontal organization**), in which employees now strive to acquire new knowledge and skills (the **learning organization**) and work in groups (**teams and teaming**). Finally the application of all these concepts and thinking will lead to organizations becoming knowledge-driven within the context of the information society. Entering the **knowledge era** will mean that organizations will need to underpin their strategies, processes and structure with **computer technology** and the **convergence of various communications systems**.

Right and left sides of the brain

We are told by experts that as far as brain hemispheres are concerned, the left hemisphere of brain controls a significant proportion of analytical mental functions and logical and rational capabilities, whereas the right hemisphere of brain accommodates intuitive and emotional elements. The left hemisphere tends to process information in a sequential manner whereas the right hemisphere tends to deal with simultaneous relationships.

Introduction

People in business (top management as well as low levels of management and employees) have to be adept at using their right and left sides of the brain. **The new management thinking reflects not only logical and rational thinking but it also incorporates emotions, trust and intuition**. Exercising both sides of the brain will bring about alignment between organizational development and goals on the one hand, and aspirations of employees and satisfaction of customers on the other.

in brief.

God grant me courage
to change the things I
can,
The patience to accept
the things I cannot
change,
And the wisdom to
know the difference.

Poet's prayer

Prologue:
Memo from the chief executive officers to all employees

To: All employees (converts, believers, agnostics and atheists)
From: Chief executive officers
Subject: Managing and living with change

The business world is changing very dramatically and we have to change accordingly if we want to survive in an intensely competitive climate. We would like to take this opportunity to outline for you the various change initiatives our companies have adopted so that you understand the reasons behind certain decisions and actions.

Total quality management

All companies are facing fierce competition. To win and retain customers we have to deliver quality goods and services. Total quality management is not a fad; it is a business reality.

We have to improve the quality of products, processes and people. Everyone in the company is responsible for total quality.

Benchmarking

We will initiate projects to benchmark different aspects of business. Some of you will be involved in benchmarking customer service, some in financial operations, marketing and sales and human resources. The main objective of benchmarking is to adopt best practice.

Customer service

Your salaries are paid by customers not companies. The way we deal with our customers and the way we treat them is going to be the key differentiating factor. We urge you to adopt an attitude 'treat others as you would wish them treat you'.

We have put in place various mechanisms to listen to our customers and to treat our suppliers as our partners. We also expect you to establish long-term relationships with our key customers.

Business process re-engineering

The latest management thinking is to focus our attention on our processes, that is the way we develop new products, the way we fulfil our orders and so on. We have formed teams to look at various processes and to suggest ways to eliminate activities that do not add value. Re-engineering could lead to job losses but in our view it is better to lose a few jobs now than to lose the whole business if we do not re-engineer.

Performance measurement

We have decided to review our measurement philosophy and approach. We will be measuring the effectiveness of all our processes and the way our people perform various roles within the companies.

Empowerment

We have recently made 200 managers and supervisors redundant in order to flatten our organizational structure. You now have to work in teams and in each team you will have a freedom to address various problems and make key decisions.

Prologue

In order to enable you to perform specialized as well as general functions within teams we have asked our human resource departments to recommend training programmes and to present the budget with their recommendations. In the absence of vertical career ladders we will institute ways of moving employees horizontally across the company so that you build portfolios of skills.

You are our greatest asset. If you can understand the reasons for various changes and the rationale behind them, we feel you will be able to give us your full commitment.

We, in turn, will try to be open and honest in our communications with you. However, you have to understand that our board from time to time may recommend cost-cutting exercises in which case we have to reduce the number of our workforce. We do, however, value your service and commitment.

1

Snapshots of the competitive environment

in brief.

"It is only when you are pursued that you become swift."
Anonymous

Summary

■ The profile of the business world is changing dramatically.

■ Businesses are affected by the external environment within which they operate. The variables in the external environment are categorized into sociological, technological, economic and political (STEP) factors. Factors within each category influence business strategy.

■ Finally, in order not only to survive in the changing business climate of the 1990s but also to be the organization of the twenty-first century, it is recommended that organizations re-think the philosophy and the role of marketing. Some experts advocate relationship marketing in order to gain, satisfy and retain customers. It is also proposed that 'business excellence' should be the focus and the core of business.

Introduction

This chapter is not about management theories or about total management thinking as such. All organizations have to operate and make decisions within the national and international or global environment. Management 'gurus' and writers have advocated adopting new management thinking in order to respond effectively to the changing sociological, economic, technological and political environment. In addition, organizations constantly have to review their positions in the competitive arena in which they are players.

The changing business world

Pioneers and gurus

In the area of competitive strategy, the person who has made a significant impact is Professor Michael Porter who teaches at Harvard Business School. He developed the widely acclaimed MBA courses on competitive strategy. His books *Competitive Strategy* (1980) and *Competitive Advantage* (1985), have become essential reading for students and executives interested in competitive strategy.

As far as external environment factors are concerned, marketing gurus like Philip Kotler and Theodore Levitt have highlighted the importance of making strategic decisions within the environmental context.

Corporate casualties

According to Professor D. Quinn Mills, today's status quo is change. The profile of the business world is changing dramatically. The history of enterprise is littered with household names which have gone out of existence. In 1986 IBM was one of the most admired companies. In 1993 IBM made a loss of $48.1 billion. The book *In Search of Excellence* by Peters and Waterman was published in 1982. It became the all-time business best seller in America. Almost half of the 43 companies selected for the 'excellence' class no longer deserve the classification.

2

What went wrong?

The following are some of the reasons which contributed to the downfall of some of the 'excellent' companies:

- Failure to read market signals.
- Arrogance.
- Rigid organizational culture.
- Bureaucracy.
- Obsession with analysing own performance to the neglect of customers.
- Ego trips.

Household names like Philips, Digital Equipment, Caterpillar, General Motors, Matsushita and the like had to restructure their organizations in order to survive. Survival in the 1990s means organizations have to be able to adapt. Organizations have to pay attention not only to the changing competitive environment but must also keep an eye on their competitors from all over the world.

Organizational effectiveness depends on how well changes in the micro-environment and macro-environment are responded to. The micro-environment consists of the industrial structure within which companies operate. The macro-environment consists of social, technological, economic and

Figure 1.1 Micro- and macro-environmental factors

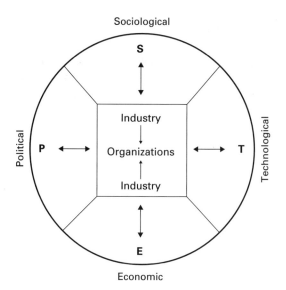

political factors (**STEP factors**) affecting business operations and strategies.

Strategic decisions are influenced by the behaviour of the competitors, the nature of the industry within which companies operate and changes in the STEP factors.

Theoretical framework – STEP factors

1 Social factors

Social factors relate to changes taking place in a society. These changes apply to social attitudes, social values, changes in the education system, life styles, structure of household, the family unit, the role of women and minorities, and so on. All these changes impact upon industrial structure and organizational strategies. Demographic changes such as birth rates, population size, age structure and population mobility affect human resources and marketing strategies of companies.

Impact of demography

If we consider the demographic factors alone it is estimated that the world population is going to grow to six billion before the end of the century. Asia will remain by far the most populous continent. Many countries will experience a trend towards smaller families as a result of changes in the socio-economic conditions. Mortality rates in all countries will fall and in regions such as the USA and Europe, the population will become increasingly aged.

Ageing populations present the global challenge. In 1990 almost 500 million people (more than 9 per cent of the world's population) were more than 60 years old. The World Bank estimates that by 2030 the number will be 1.4 billion and that most of the growth will take place in developing countries and specifically in Asia.

The World Bank points out that while it took more than 100 years for the share of the population over 60 in Belgium to double from 9 to 18 per cent, the same transition will take only

4

34 years in China and 22 years in Venezuela. Developing countries will have elderly demographic profiles at much lower levels of per capita income than the leading industrialized countries.

In India, with a population of over 900 million (1994), economic growth will lead to the creation of an urban middle-class with both the ability and desire to buy consumer goods and services. Over 50 per cent of India's gross domestic product (GDP) is currently accounted for by 180 million urban dwellers. Of these, 30–40 million have consumption patterns similar to those of the West.

The Green revolution

Society is also concerned about environmental and ecological factors such as emission and safety standards, recycling and pollution levels. Products are coming to the market which are labelled as 'environmentally friendly' in order to respond to the desires of the customers. In the early 1990s some computer printer manufacturers started to market environmental aspects of their products such as recycled paper and the use of toner containers capable of being burned.

Some organizations consider environmental indicators as one of the key measures of their performance. At the second World Industry Conference on Environmental Management held in Rotterdam in April 1991, there were more than 700 leading industrialists present to discuss key environmental issues for industry. The environment is becoming just another part of a business manager's legitimate day-to-day concern.

The introduction of the Eco-Audit Management Scheme (EMAS) throughout the European Union has added an extra dimension for companies seeking to use management systems in order to raise environmental awareness and improve business performance. EMAS is a voluntary scheme aimed at improving the environmental performance of companies. To achieve recognition companies must develop an environmental management system and prepare a public environmental statement. Both must be then validated by an independent accredited certification body.

BS 7750 is the UK standard for defining the scope and contents of an organization's Environmental Management System (EMS). It is currently the only EMS standard available

Management Ideas

and applicable world-wide. The standard is voluntary and consists of the following five elements:

- Developing an environmental policy.
- Evaluating environmental effects.
- Setting overall goals and specific measurable targets.
- Establishing management control.
- Reviewing the system regularly.

BS 7750 is applicable world-wide whereas EMAS applies only to organizations within the European Union.

The *Financial Times* on 31 May 1995 reported Vauxhall, the UK arm of the US company General Motors, as the first recipient of an award for environmental management. Vauxhall's Ellesmere Port plant has become the first car factory to receive the BS 7750 award for the environment management from the British Standards Institution. It acknowledges the management's environmental awareness. Shopfloor staff were trained and the environmental responsibility was shifted to the senior staff. Ten environmental auditors were appointed to monitor environmental progress. Most of the changes involved eliminating waste and reducing energy consumption.

The article 'Greening the bottom line' published in *Management Today* in July, 1995, mentions how Nissan, the Japanese car company, is attempting to become environmentally friendly: 'the most vivid example of Nissan's policy in action is the way that money saved by recycling plastic off-cuts from the manufacture of Micra and Primera fuel tanks is paying for the switch to environmentally friendly (but more expensive) water-based paints on the Micra to reduce solvent emissions.'

The same article goes on to say that several of the most environmentally conscious companies have been using their clout to try to encourage environmental friendliness in their suppliers. According to KPMG, one of the leading management consultancies, in 1994, 34 per cent of the *Financial Times'* top 100 companies produced separate environmental reports compared with only 20 per cent in 1993.

According to Sandra Mullins of British Standards Institution, the formal publication of ISO 14000 will introduce a third option for organizations to implement an environmental management system. The formal standards were published at the end of 1996.

National considerations

Within the sociological factors also come differences in national cultures. Understanding the mentalities and histories of particular societies have also become important in managing at cross-border level. In every culture, authority, bureaucracy, creativity, empowerment and downsizing are experienced in different ways. Often management techniques with standardized jargons taken from one culture fail when they are taken across borders.

The most widely known research in the field of culture is the pioneering work of Geert Hofstede. His research covered 53 countries within a single organization, IBM. He concluded that there are four work-related dimensions on which cultures differ. These dimensions were power/distance (distribution of power in society), uncertainty avoidance, individualism versus collectivism and masculinity versus femininity (society's endorsement of masculine and feminine qualities).

Another description of how cultures differ has been developed by the Dutch economist and consultant, Fons Trompenaars. His research revealed seven dimensions of culture. His findings facilitate the most practical way for managers to consider how cultural differences influence their organizations.

Cultural differences

Understanding differences in national cultures helps organizations become effective in negotiations, selection, team work, performance management, empowerment and adopting an appropriate management style.

In a recent report published by Anglo-German Foundation, the findings highlight differences in managing in Britain and in Germany. German managers desire control over uncertainty and they rely on inter-personal formality, punctuality, consistency and order, dependability and trust, team spirit and co-operation. In Britain the managers focus on commitment, initiative, ownership, responsibility, personal sense of accomplishment and coaching.

If one takes an example of negotiation, for example in Japanese and American contexts, the Japanese team will consist of many delegates (focus on collectivism), they arrive at decisions by consensus, they are generally polite and value trust. The American team, on the other hand, will consist of few delegates, the decisions will be made by majority vote, they will be assertive and focus on legal agreement. According to Michael Porter 'National differences in character and culture, far from being threatened by global competition, prove integral to the success of it.'

2 Technological factors

New technologies and skills are becoming increasingly diffused world-wide and more and more businesses are becoming high tech. For example. South Korean companies were renowned for producing cheap shoes and textiles. Now they are becoming leading producers of high-tech goods. The push is led by Samsung, Hyundai and Daewoo.

Advances in telecommunications and computing

Technological developments are taking place at breathtaking pace, specifically in the telecommunications and entertainment industries. Advances in technologies such as personal communications systems/personal communications networks (PCSs/PCNs) and low grade orbiting satellite systems (LEOs) will intensify competition. Faster switching is allowing almost unlimited quantities of information to travel at an accelerating speed.

Optical fibres are circling the globe, enabling the realization of the global information infrastructure. Satellite technology is creating a 'global broadcasting system'. It is predicted that almost all the major countries in the Asia Pacific region will be linked by optical fibre submarine cable systems by the end of this century.

Several dominant technologies are converging which are shaping the telecommunications industry. These technologies are fibre optic radio, ATM (asynchronous transfer mode) and low cost computing. These technologies are being deployed concurrently. The convergence of computing, communications and information will lead to a global information superhighway which will expand markets, develop new businesses and increase competition. Some say 'the future is not what it used to be'.

Everyone is familiar with the Internet and yet a decade ago it was unthinkable that an international network could grow from 1 million to 30 million users in less than four years. New technologies and their falling costs have become the important catalysts in changing the way business is being organized. We are now witnessing collaborative technological projects being undertaken with rivals. For example, Texas Instruments and Hitachi Ltd, NEC and AT&T and Intel and Sharp. According to Lawrie Philpott of Coopers & Lybrand 'individually and corporately we will have to learn how to deal in a marketspace rather than marketplace.' One must also remember that the faster rate of technological breakthroughs makes organizational uniqueness obsolete very quickly.

Technology has also been the main driver behind flexible working. It is estimated that the cost of providing an office-based desk in the UK is about £6000 per annum. Many organizations such as Anderson Consulting and Digital Equipment Co. are investigating more cost-effective ways of managing their operations.

According to a survey commissioned by Digital, more than half of their salesforce, service staff and consultants spend less than 40 per cent of their time in the office. Facts like this are prompting companies to analyse how people work within their organization. Equipped with modems, fax machines and mobile telephones, some employees are involved in flexible work practices. Some companies develop environments where work is performed in the most effective way at home, in community offices and in 'tele-cottages'.

Flexible working will increase in the twenty-first century. It is important to consider a careful integration of business needs, people needs and technology. More and more people will opt for home-based working and advances in multimedia are facilitating such needs.

3 Economic factors

The economic landscape is also changing dramatically. Key economic variables such as wealth, purchasing power, inflation, unemployment, interest rates, exchange rates, growth, investment and savings are all key determinants of demand. One of the most sensitive issues for many businesses today is the level of interest rates. The late 1980s and early 1990s saw high levels of interest rates in

Management Ideas

many European countries. Interest rates increase as soon as there is an indication of inflation rates increasing. Interest rates affect the servicing of loans, levels of capital expenditure, housing finance, movement of 'hot' money, savings and investment.

Another key economic factor impacting on competition is exchange rates. Fluctuations in exchange rates affect exports and imports. Discussions are still going on in relation to fixing of exchange rate fluctuations within the European Union and the introduction of the single currency.

The past two decades have also seen revolution as domestic financial markets have been opened up to create a massive global capital market. This change has contributed to the explosive growth of the financial markets. A free capital market ensures that savings are directed to the most productive investments without regard for national boundaries.

Most economists predict that the fastest growing economies will be South East Asia and Japan. Economic growth in Europe and the USA is likely to remain sluggish. The annual percentage increase in the gross domestic product of the UK, Italy, France and Germany, for example, is forecasted to be under 3 per cent in 1997. The North American Free Trade (NAFTA) and the completion of the GATT Uruguay Round will provide a boost to world trade volumes. The high spots for growth in the European economy are in Central and Eastern Europe. In Hungary, Poland, the Czech Republic and Slovakia, a rapid growth is already establishing itself.

As far as the Asian economies are concerned Korea, Taiwan, Singapore and Hong Kong are expected to gain a significant increase in the world share of manufactured exports. The share of the world output held by all the Asian developing economies is likely to increase from one-fifth in 1990 to nearly one-third by 2010. Many analysts believe India is poised to become economically one of the key 'Asian tigers' by the end of the century. Her open policy on inward motor industry investment has attracted the US's General Motors, Germany's Daimler Benz, Fiat of Italy and Peugeot of France to an expanding Indian market.

4 Political factors

Politically the climate is changing from conflict to co-operation. Geographic boundaries are ceasing to be barriers to competition. State-owned businesses are being sold and markets are being liberalized. Many countries are emulating the success of the privatization and deregulation policies of the UK and the USA. Privatization and deregulation are becoming the major internal sources of new competition.

Since the fall of the Berlin Wall and the abandonment of communism there have been steady streams of acquisitions and alliances and strategic partnerships and supplier networks. The global shrinkage is the result of not only advances in technology and communication but also of changing political ideologies. Former communist and socialist countries are opening up their markets and are creating an infrastructure to compete with industrially advanced countries. On 26 July 1995, an international accord on liberalizing trade in financial services was completed after Japan and South Korea joined other countries in committing themselves to improving access to the markets. This accord (the Geneva Accord) will cover an estimated 90 per cent of the financial services market. Indonesia, Thailand, Malaysia and other Asian countries offered attractive prospects in life and health insurance, with China and Vietnam among those which would develop later.

China has initiated the creation of a 'socialist market economy'. In March 1993 the overall concept of socialist market economy was embedded in China's constitution. In such a market structure central management of the economy is replaced by market forces. Special economic zones were created in which liberalized policies are tried. The first securities exchanges opened in Shanghai and Shenzen. Nation-wide electronic trading systems for securities including treasuries were also initiated. In 1993 the Central Committee of the Communist Party of China in its 'Decision on Economic Structure' reaffirmed its commitment to a wide spectrum of market-based economies. Similar developments are taking place in Vietnam, Cuba and the Philippines.

Influence of STEP factors on business organizations

■ Changing political ideologies and a climate of co-operation have facilitated 'borderless organizations'. Thomson, the French consumer electronics giant, is making TV tubes in Poland. Ireland's Waterford Wedgwood plc is producing its crystals in Hungary. German businesses are shifting some of their operations to Slovakia and Slovenia. Audi has operations in Hungary, Siemens in Poland and Volkswagen has a 25 per cent stake in the Czech car maker Skoda. NEC, the largest semiconductor manufacturer in the world, is opening a plant in Scotland. In June 1994 Hyundai Electronics announced plans to invest $1.3 billion in a semiconductor plant in Oregon. Intel has opened a semiconductor plant in Ireland and is now expanding production in California, Arizona and New Mexico. And the story of 'borderless' organization and production continues.

■ Central Europe is becoming the manufacturing zone for European businesses. The workers in these countries are hitting quality and productivity standards on a par with their Western counterparts. Central European countries are aligning their trade, legal and economic systems to those of the West.

■ Toyota, Japan's leading car maker, announced in July 1995 that it wants to double its total production outside Japan by the end of the century. The main growth in overseas production will come in North America and South East Asia. Toyota also hopes to establish more plants in Canada, Argentina, the United Kingdom, Thailand, the Philippines and hopefully in China and Vietnam.

■ Toshiba has plants in South East Asia and China. In both China and Vietnam joint ventures are becoming the order of the day for multinationals. BP Petco for example, in Vietnam, is 65 per cent owned by BP and 35 per cent by Petrolimax, the local state-owned oil company.

■ Pepsi expects to have US$1 billion committed to China by 2000. Pepsi also bought three of the top eight brands in China and has a commitment to bottle up to 30 per cent local brands at its joint venture bottling plants.

■ In November 1994 Ciba Geigy opened its fifteenth operation in China. The company at present has 1050 staff in China and US$270 million in capital commitments.

Snapshots of the competitive environment

■ Royal Dutch Shell, the Anglo-Dutch oil company, plans to move a regional HQ to Beijing by the end of 1997, when Hong Kong is due to be handed back to China.

■ Philips is moving more and more of its electronics business to South East Asia. Hoechst, the German chemical company, has shifted the bulk of its genetic research to the USA. Electrolux has a research laboratory in Finland, a development centre in Sweden and a design group in Italy. Skills and knowledge are now being managed across borders.

■ Agreements have been finalized between Hindustan Motors and Mitsubishi of Japan to make Mitsubishi's Lancer model in India by 1997.

The latest cross-border globalization story is that of Texas Instruments' high speed telecommunications chip which was conceived by engineers from Ericsson Telephone Co. in Sweden, designed in Nice with software tools the company developed in Houston. According to *Business Week* (7 August 1995), 'Today's TCM 9055 chip rolls off production lines in Japan and Dallas, gets tested in Taiwan and is wired into Ericsson line-cards that monitor phone systems in Sweden, the US, Mexico and Australia.'

In response to STEP factors organizations are becoming increasingly 'borderless' and such ventures will continue throughout the 1990s. According to Professor Quinn Mills, 'The new competition is contributing to a renaissance in the fundamentals of management.'

Changing competitive climates favour 'the survival of the fittest'. To become the fittest organizations have to be agile and responsive to customers' needs. Even when they think they have the right strategy they need constantly and continuously to review their operation. As someone said, 'Being on the right track is not enough. If you do not move fast and in the right direction you will be taken over or run over'.

A good example to illustrate how organizations respond to market needs is to examine the decision of AT&T to disintegrate in order to enhance its responsiveness to market needs. On 20 September 1995, AT&T chairman Robert Allen announced that the corporation's different businesses will be split and listed on the New York Stock Exchange. One entry will be AT&T Communications and will include the card service and systems integration businesses. A second entry will cover AT&T's research and development arm, while the third will cover the corporation's network and business communications system and microelectronics. AT&T is also pulling out of the manufacture of personal computers as part of a bid to scale back its global information systems division and spin it off.

According to Robert Allen, transformation of AT&T is due to customer needs, technology and public policy. The move to demerge makes a sharp reversal of policy for a company that has preached the virtues of 'big is beautiful' for more than 100 years.

Analysing your business

Under each category – namely, social, technological, economic and political – identify key variables and assess their probability of change and the consequent impact of that change on your operations in terms of cost, revenue or profitability (see Figure 1.2). All the factors in the high-high box should be analysed in detail and taken on board to formulate your business strategy.

Figure 1.2 Impact analysis (economic factors)

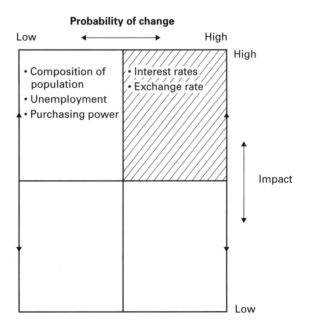

Too much analysis leads to paralysis

However, organizations should not become too obsessed with analysing the competitive environment and competitors because the business environment is changing all the time. Totally unexpected competitors can enter the market and frustrate their strategies. AT&T never considered oil haulier Williams Co. to be a competitor until one day Williams Co. decided to use their pipelines to carry fibreoptic cables. Many big organizations like Marks & Spencer, for example, offer financial services. Should banks consider them as key competitors? It is said that General Motors is really a bank that uses cars as an incentive. Now some mortgage lenders offer expensive cars as incentives if you take out loans with them. Too much internal analysis can lead to the organization's downfall. Remember, 'The downfall of a magician is the belief in his own magic'.

Having done the analysis of competition and competitors, organizations then have to take necessary actions to position themselves in the global marketplace. In 1994 IBM decided to restructure its world-wide marketing and sales, manufacturing and engineering operations in order to take advantage of global markets. Other companies who have undertaken similar reorganizations to position themselves in competitive global markets were Bristol-Meyer Squibb Co., Ford, General Electric, AT&T, Hewlett–Packard, Toyota and even ABB, which carved its global operations into three super-regional groups for Europe, the Americas and Asia, folding six industrial divisions into four. According to Percy Barnevik, the CEO of ABB, organizations these days have to manage 'perpetual revolution'.

Another action plan would be to focus on core activities and processes and outsource other functions. Outsourcing nowadays has become an important way of enabling organizations to remain responsive to market needs.

According to Tom Peters everything can be outsourced. Outsourcing at present takes place in activities such as catering, cleaning, computing, logistics, and so on. Some companies even outsource the research and development function. Outsourcing R&D is more common among Japanese companies than US or European companies.

Outsourcing

Outsourcing is not taken for purely 'off-loading' reasons. Companies now make outsourcing decisions on a strategic basis. Few companies can cope with the increasing costs of keeping up with a large number of different technologies. Outsourcing of any function or operation should be a part of an overall strategic framework which takes corporate objectives into account. Outside such a strategic framework, outsourcing will remain an 'ad hoc' response to circumstances driven by cost minimization and downsizing.

Reviewing the philosophy of marketing

Finally, in light of changing business profile and the ways organizations respond to the changing environment the time has come for organizations to review their marketing function. Like organizations, **marketing needs to reinvent itself**. It was Peter Drucker who a long time ago said that marketing is not an appendix to an organization. **Marketing is business and business is marketing**. Why is it then we are reluctant to move from the old concept of marketing?

The basic definition and functions of marketing have remained unchanged in many educational and training syllabi. Marketing is about understanding and meeting customer needs and maintaining customer loyalty. This is as true today as it was in the 1950s and 1960s when we were studying marketing. What, however, has changed is the nature of the customers.

Today's customers

Customers now have a wide variety of choice. They have become educated and sophisticated. The Japanese products did well in the West because customers found out that Japanese goods did not mean shoddy goods. Consumers became discriminating customers. Japanese companies truly understood how to win customers globally, whereas in the West the concept of marketing has not changed but most importantly the approach has not changed much either. In an effort to make companies and organizations market-focused, organizations are undergoing total quality management, delayering, downsizing, restructuring, re-engineering and transformation. Some organizations have embarked upon relationship marketing. Employees are being grouped into multi-tasking teams and empowered, and we are told top management is becoming more enlightened.

The road to business excellence

Organizational restructuring – focusing attention on products, processes and people

The core objective of marketing should still be to understand and to satisfy customers but today's marketers should be well conversant with the ways to win and retain customers and enable organizations to attain this objective. The marketing department should be abolished and in its place we should have a department of business excellence. This department would focus its attention on the three Ps – product, processes and people.

An aspect of this department should look at the products that customers want and those that customers *could* want. Attention should be paid to creativity and innovation. The other aspect should be the processes which organizations undertake in order to produce these products. The department should focus on value-adding activities in each process. The people aspect should be divided into employees and customers. The department will be responsible for fostering very good inter-personal relationships within the organization. This aspect will take on board selection, training, communication and 'internal customers' perspectives. Finally external customers would involve suppliers, distributors and customers.

Management Ideas

The core of the organization structure should be the business excellence department consisting of multi-skilled individuals. The board of management should be dominated by business excellence champions. The main functions of the director of business excellence should be to align the operational and peoples objectives to corporate objectives and customer needs to corporate strategy.

Relationship marketing

The term 'relationship marketing' has been talked about and written about for a number of years. Various articles have appeared in the professional journals focusing attention on creating customer value.

Relationship marketing calls for customer-orientated production and delivery of services and products. Database technology enables companies to gather huge amounts of data on individual customers' needs and preferences. Companies that create relationships with their customers will be able to retain them for a very long time. 'Keeping customers for life' seems to be the main marketing cry today.

According to Fredrick Reichheld of Bain & Co. 'Raising customer retention rates by five percentage points increases the value of an average customer by 25 per cent to 100 per cent'. Also the retained customer costs less to service than the cost of acquiring new customers, though winning new customers is important as well.

What is the difference between relationship marketing and traditional marketing?

Adrian Payne, Martin Christopher, Moira Clark and Helen Peck have written a very readable book entitled *Relationship Marketing for Competitive Advantage* (1995). They have contrasted traditional marketing which they call 'transactional approach' to relationship marketing. The following is an extract from their book:

Transactional focus	Relationship focus
Orientation to single sales	Orientation to
Discontinuous customer contact	customer retention
Focus on product features	Continuous customer
Short time scale	contact
Little emphasis on customer service	Focus on customer value
Limited commitment to meeting	Long time scale
customer expectations	High customer service emphasis.
Quality is the concern of production	High commitment to meeting
	customer expectations
	Quality is the concern of all staff

Examples of relationship marketing

■ Mr Bloggs bought a multimedia computer for £2500 from distributor A. Two months later A got in touch with Bloggs to find out if he was satisfied with the purchase and to inform him not to hesitate to contact them if there was any problem or if he wanted more information. The store also assured him not to worry and to keep in touch with them even after expiry of the warranty.

■ The store kept in touch with Bloggs. After two years Bloggs decided to upgrade the system. He dealt with A. What is more he encouraged all his relatives and friends to deal with A thus generating additional revenue for A.

■ A manufacturer of cat food has all the details of its customers including the number of cats, their names and their birthdays on its database. The company sends birthday cards to their key customers' cats. They thus maintain a good relationship with their customers.

In his interview with the editor of the *European Management Journal*, December 1994, Philip Kotler said, 'Companies have shifted their focus from customer attraction to customer retention. Customer retention requires knowing much more about a customer, as might be captured in a marketing database. The company's task is not to make a sale but to build loyal customers. Marketing is the company's manufacturing department and relationship marketing is the key.'

For relationship marketing to succeed organizations must have:

Management Ideas

(a) capacity to deliver;

(b) information on their customers;

(c) staff who understand the value of relationships with their customers.

In other words, the main drivers of relationship marketing are a good database, a personalized approach, integrated functions and a customer-focused mindset. The four Ps of traditional marketing (product, place, promotion and price) have to be replaced with four Cs – customer, communication, conviction and commitment – in order to retain customers and sustain their loyalty.

Do organizations have a choice?

There have been dramatic changes in the STEP factors. Companies must reorient their entire business to face the market. In the past few years many organizations have undergone transformation in order to be responsive to market needs. Various functions have become integrated in order to break out from 'compartmentalized thinking'. Marketing requires a new philosophy and marketers have to adopt a new mindset.

According to Mack Hanan, a consultant, 'Marketing has been advertised as an instrument of warfare against our competitors, rather than an instrument of welfare helping customers'.

The rest of the book examines how companies have operationalized management theories and thinking in order to be close to their customers and survive in a fierce competitive climate.

Selected reading

Joseph L. Bower (1986) *When Markets Quake*. Harvard Business School Press.

Joan Cannie and Donald Caplin (1991) *Keeping Customers for Life*. American Management Association.

Peter F. Drucker (1986) *The Frontiers of Management*. Butterworth–Heinemann.

Peter F. Drucker (1992) *Managing for the Future*. Butterworth–Heinemann.

Peter F. Drucker (1995) *Managing in a Time of Great Change*. Butterworth–Heinemann.

The Economist Intelligence Unit (1993) *Managing Cultural Differences for Competitive Advantage*.

European Management Journal (1994) Philip Kotler Interview. December.

D. Quinn Mills (1985) *The New Competitors*. John Wiley & Sons.

Adrian Payne, Martin Christopher, Maria Clark and Helen Peck (1995) *Relationship Marketing for Competitive Advantage*. Butterworth–Heinemann.

Tom Peters and Robert Waterman Jr. (1982) *In Search of Excellence*. Harper & Row.

Tom Peters (1988) *Thriving on Chaos*. Alfred A. Knopf.

Michael E. Porter (1980) *Competitive Strategy*. The Free Press.

Michael E. Porter (1985) *Competitive Advantage*. The Free Press.

Robert H. Waterman, Jr. (1987) *The Renewal Factor*. Bantam Books.

2 Total quality management

in brief

"We are what we
repeatedly do.
Excellence, then, is not
an act, but a habit."
Aristotle

Summary

■ Total quality management was one of the most pervasive aspects of management thinking of the 1980s.

■ Product and service quality has been part of marketing teaching for a number of years. What is so different about total quality management?

■ The influence of Juran, Deming and Crosby – the 'gurus' of total quality.

■ The seven basic tools of quality management: control charts, Pareto charts, cause and effect diagrams, bar charts, histograms, scatter diagrams and flow charts.

■ Quality functional deployment (QFD) – listening to the voice of the customer.

■ Quality awards: the Deming Prize, the Baldrige Award, and the European Quality Award.

■ ISO 9000 – reasons for obtaining certifications, expectations and benefits.

■ TQM success stories: Rank Xerox, ICL and Miliken Industrials.

■ Reasons for companies failing in spite of going through quality initiatives – how not to fail.

■ Quality soundbites of the 1990s.

■ How to make your organization a quality master.

Total quality management

Total quality management (TQM) was one of the most pervasive aspects of management thinking of the 1980s. Many
experts believe that those organizations who want to remain
profitable and achieve competitive advantage in the 1990s
have to go through the TQM journey. The cornerstone of TQM
is customer satisfaction. Without focus on customers, TQM
becomes a futile and expensive exercise.

Products and customers

The link between a product and the customer's perception of
it is not new thinking. Philip Kotler, a well known author on
marketing, defined a product as 'anything that can be offered
to a market for attention, acquisition, use, or consumption that
might satisfy a want or need. It includes physical objects,
services, persons, places, organizations and ideas'.

In developing or designing a product, the planner has to
think about the product at three levels. The first level is the
'core product' level incorporating all the benefits to the
consumers. The second is the 'tangible product' level. At this
level the product assumes the characteristics of quality,
features, packaging, styling and brand name. Finally the
product planner has to enhance the benefits and make up an
'augmented product'. At this stage benefits are enhanced to
meet customer needs and aspirations in relation to that

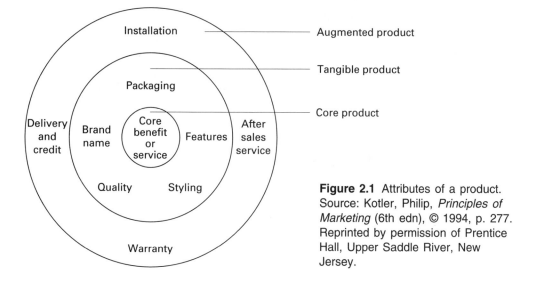

Figure 2.1 Attributes of a product.
Source: Kotler, Philip, *Principles of
Marketing* (6th edn), © 1994, p. 277.
Reprinted by permission of Prentice
Hall, Upper Saddle River, New
Jersey.

product. Kotler argued that 'consumers perceive the product as a complex bundle of benefits that satisfy needs. . .'

Another marketing guru, Theodore Levitt, was also an advocate of looking beyond the physical attributes of a product and focusing attention on adding value to the product to meet customer needs. In the 1970s and early 1980s the cry was to listen to the voice of the marketplace and to add value to a product.

While in marketing terms 'value added' became the buzz word of the 1980s, especially after Michael Porter reinforced the concept of the value chain in 1980, total quality was taking over some of the boardrooms of the US companies. The enthusiasm for quality came about because many businesses were finding it hard to compete with Japanese products. In the 1950s and 1960s Japan acquired the reputation of copycat country and shoddy mimicry. In the 1970s and 1980s Japan acquired a reputation for producing goods that delighted customers. Soon Japanese goods penetrated Western home markets in cars and electronic consumer goods. Hand in hand while marketing gurus were redefining the concept of a product to be more responsive to customer needs, US businesses decided to embark upon the TQM initiative in order to remain competitive.

What is TQM?

TQM is concerned with continuous improvement in performance aimed at delighting customers. These are some of the definitions put forward:

- ■ 'Achieving total quality through gaining everyone's commitment and involvement.'
- ■ 'Improvement of the quality of the organization's products and services for the customers.'
- ■ 'Customer-oriented, continuous improvement process.'
- ■ 'Quality is conformance to requirements.'
- ■ 'Fitness for use.'

Whichever definition we examine the two things that stand out are **customer** and **continuous improvement**. The word 'total' is designed to send the message that all processes, systems, all levels of management and all employees must be concerned with quality. 'Quality is everyone's business'.

Who are the gurus of total quality?

There are numerous gurus dealing with different aspects of quality management. But we will deal with three of them, namely, Juran, Deming and Crosby.

Joseph M. Juran

Juran was born in December 1904 in Braita, Romania and emigrated to the USA in 1912. For almost 50 years he has remained a leading proponent of quality. From the 1950s he advised Japanese senior and supervisory management on a broad range of management issues as well as writing several seminal books on quality.

His significant contribution was his formulation of methods for creating a customer-oriented organization. Achieving quality, he emphasized throughout his career, is about communication, management commitment and people.

Juran offers the following implementation framework to any organization setting out to establish total quality:

Juran's ten steps to quality improvement

1. Build awareness of the need for quality and an opportunity for improvement.
2. Set goals for improvement.
3. Organize to achieve goals.
4. Provide training.
5. Carry out projects to solve problems.
6. Report progress.
7. Give recognition.
8. Communicate results.
9. Keep score.
10. Maintain momentum.

Source: Various writings of Juran. Also Course B889, the Open University Business School

Management Ideas

In his ten steps, Juran highlights the need to plan, set targets for improvement, organize for implementation and then highlights the training, communications and recognition aspects of quality. To put such a system into practice requires 'total' commitment and understanding from top management to all levels of management and operations.

Juran received several awards including Japan's Order of the Sacred Treasure, conferred in 1981 by Emperor Hirohito. It took the USA a very long time to appreciate Juran's message on quality. Why was this the case?

■ Most senior managers in the USA were almost entirely focused on finance and short term financial performance.
■ International competition in the early stages was not posing any threats to US businesses. US businesses after the Second World War were working in a 'comfortable' climate. As Tom Peters would say, 'even if they had tried they could not have done wrong'.
■ Quality was delegated to functional departments. It was a 'nitty-gritty' aspect of business whereas captains of industry only dealt with strategic issues.
■ Most top management had their heads buried in the sand.

W. Edwards Deming

Deming believed that quality must be the foundation of everything businesses do. He was born in October 1900 and died in December 1993. As a graduate in mathematics and physics he worked at the Hawthorne Plant of Western Electric Co. in 1925. While there he came in contact with Walter Shewhart who pioneered statistical quality work. He later worked with the US Department of Agriculture and the National Bureau of the Census.

In 1950 he was invited by Japanese scientists and engineers to address them. This was followed by a meeting with 21 Japanese companies including such names as Nissan, Toyota and Sony. He showed the Japanese how they could improve quality by the use of the statistical control of processes. He is considered by many to be the father of the Japanese quality revolution.

A consistent theme in Deming's work has been the reluctance of managers to accept that theirs is the key role in changing processes and driving the improvement in quality. He developed a very simple method of problem solving which is now known as the Deming cycle. The cycle (Figure 2.2) has four stages namely, plan, do, check and action. Deming also developed 14 points for successful total quality management.

Figure 2. 2 The Deming cycle

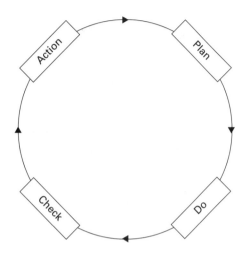

Deming's 14 points for management

1. Create constancy for the purpose of improvement of product and service. Allocate resources to provide for long-term needs with a view to becoming competitive.
2. Adopt the new philosophy. We are in a new economic age. We can no longer live with mistakes and defects. Western management must awaken to the challenge, must learn their responsibilities and take on leadership for change.
3. Eliminate dependence on mass inspection. Quality must be built into the product. Quality must be the foundation on which the organization is based.
4. Eliminate awarding business based on price alone. Instead minimize total cost. Move toward a single supplier for any one item, on a long-term relationship of loyalty and trust.
5. Improve constantly and forever the system of production and service, to improve quality and productivity and thus constantly decreasing costs. What is good enough for today is not good enough for tomorrow.

6. Institute training on the job.
7. Institute leadership. The aim of supervision would be to help people and machines do a better job. Supervision of management is in need of overhaul, as well as supervision of production workers.
8. Drive out fear. Create a climate in which everyone may work effectively for the company.
9. Break down barriers between departments. People in research, design, sales and production must work as a team to tackle problems encountered with the product or service.
10. Eliminate slogans and exhortations and targets for the workforce asking for zero defects and new levels of productivity. Such exhortations only create adversarial relationships, as the bulk of the causes of low quality and low productivity belong to the system and thus lie beyond the power of the workforce.
11. Eliminate work standards (quotas). Eliminate management by numbers and numerical goals.
12. Eliminate barriers to pride of workmanship. This implies, inter alia, abolition of the annual or merit rating and of management by objectives. The responsibility of supervisors must be changed from sheer numbers to quality.
13. Institute a vigorous programme of education and self-improvement. Workers should be educated to use tools and techniques of quality as well as develop new methods of working in teams.
14. Take action to accomplish transformation. The transformation is everybody's job.

Reprinted from *Out of Crisis* by W. Edwards Deming by permission of MIT and the W. Edwards Deming Institute. Published by MIT, Center for Advanced Educational Services, Cambridge, MA 02139. Copyright 1986 by the W. Edwards Deming Institute.

Deming's 14 points constitute his basic principles of management philosophy which is sometimes referred to as his 'operational theory of management'. His 14 points taken together assume a holistic approach to quality management.

Philip B. Crosby

Philip Crosby gained prominence with the 'zero defects' movement in the 1960s. His quality improvement process is based on the following 'absolutes':

■ Quality means conformance to requirements, not goodness.
■ Quality is achieved through prevention not appraisal.
■ The performance standard is 'zero defects'.
■ The only performance measurement is the price of non-conformance.

Like Deming, Crosby also formulated the following 14 steps to quality.

Crosby's 14 steps to quality

1. Make it clear that management is committed to quality.
2. Form quality improvement teams with senior representatives from each department.
3. Determine where current and potential quality problems lie.
4. Evaluate the cost of quality and explain its use as a management tool.
5. Raise the quality awareness and personal concern of all employees.
6. Take actions to correct problems identified through previous steps.
7. Establish a committee for the zero defects programme.
8. Train supervisors to carry out their part of the quality improvement programme.
9. Hold a 'zero defects day' to let all employees realize there has been a change.
10. Encourage individuals to establish improvement goals for themselves and their groups.
11. Encourage employees to communicate to management the obstacles they face in attaining their improvement goals.
12. Recognize and appreciate those who participate.
13. Establish quality councils to communicate on a regular basis.
14. Do it all over again to emphasize that the quality improvement programme never ends.

Source: P. Crosby *Quality Without Tears* (1984). McGraw-Hill, New York.

Management Ideas

Like Juran and Deming, Crosby places the greatest responsibility for quality on management and he emphasizes the fact that all levels in the organization should receive appropriate quality education.

Crosby is an exponent of the 'zero defects' principle. Juran was a fierce critic of this principle because he believed that a significant proportion of imperfections are due to poorly designed manufacturing systems that workers cannot change. However, Crosby's 'zero defects' principle has been misunderstood and for a number of years he was at pains to explain it. In his book *Let's Talk Quality* (1989) published by McGraw-Hill he wrote, 'I learned that whenever I come up with what seems like a good idea, it is an even better idea not to spread it around until I know how best to explain it to people.' Zero defects has become a symbolic way of saying 'do it right the first time'.

Apart from the three 'gurus' mentioned, three other individuals have been influential. Armand V. Feigenbaum wrote a book entitled *Total Quality Control* (1961) which is considered by some quality engineers as a bible. Professor Ishikawa was the originator of the Ishikawa or 'fishbone' cause and effect diagram and proponent of the 'seven basic tools' of quality management. Genichi Taguchi, a Japanese engineering specialist, advocated the method of analysing quality known as 'total loss function'.

Quality circles

One of the most publicized aspect of the Japanese approach to quality has been quality circles. When Deming went to Japan in 1946 to offer advice on re-industrialization he advocated that it was not necessary to have 'specialists' in order to have quality control. The idea gave birth to quality circles in 1962, an invention of Professor Ishikawa.

The main objective of the quality circles was to encourage volunteer workers to find ways to improve processes. The onus of improving quality and to come up with the suggestions for improvements was put on workers.

In many Western organizations, where 'quality circles' were seen as a quick fix, such circles mushroomed. The growth rate of quality circles during the 1980s has been phenomenal. The quality circles consisted of a group of volunteers, between five and twelve, who worked for the same supervisors and who met regularly in normal working time under the leadership of their supervisors to identify, analyse and solve their work-related problems. They were expected to recommend solutions to management.

Even though the quality circles were very popular in Japan, it was not until the mid-1970s that US companies became active in introducing quality circles in their organizations. The quality circles appeared in companies like Lockheed Missiles, an aerospace company of California, Westinghouse, Harvey Davidson and General Motors. By 1980 quality circles became a world-wide movement. It is estimated that in the early 1980s there were one million quality circles and ten million members.

By the mid to late 1980s the quality circles began to lose their enthusiasm and excitement. First of all there was a lack of resources allocated to make such ventures successful. Time was the most important resource. Secondly top management expected quality circles to deliver quick results; this did not happen. Thirdly most members felt that in many cases the suggestions for improvements they were making were not being taken on board for a variety of reasons. In some cases the facilitators were not adequately trained. Some companies also began quality circles programmes without any real understanding of the nature of the concept. For some, forming quality circles was purely a window dressing exercise. As Juran and Deming always said, the success of any quality initiative depends on total commitment and understanding.

Quality and the customers – quality functional deployment

Quality functional deployment (QFD) is the technique of getting designers to listen to the voice of the customer. The approach, which enables designers to take into consideration consumers' needs, was pioneered by Professor Yoji Akao and Shigeru Mizuno.

A matrix is used to set product characteristics and attributes against customer needs. (Figure 2.3)

Management Ideas

Figure 2.3 How QFD works in relation to a product. There is a very strong correlation between attribute 4 of the product and customer need A, attribute 1 and customer needs B and C, attribute 2 and customer need E and attribute 5 and customer need D. In this case all five attributes of Product 'X' are important for all customers' needs.

Product 'X' attributes

Customers' needs*	ATT 1	ATT 2	ATT 3	ATT 4	ATT 5
A	0	0	0	5	0
B	5	3	2	3	0
C	5	2	2	3	3
D	2	1	2	0	5
E	1	5	1	0	0

*Information from surveys, market research, salesforce, etc.

Scoring: Strong correlation = 5
Weak correlation = 1
No correlation = 0

Quality awards

Deming Prize

The Deming Prize is named after W. Edwards Deming who set off Japan's post-1945 quality revolution. This award was created in 1951 and became Japan's most coveted industrial award. The Deming competition is run by the Japanese Union of Scientists and Engineers (JUSE). Total quality control became a pre-requisite for winning this award. Komatssu Ltd was the first winner and Toyota Motor Corporation was the second winner in 1965 under the revised guidelines incorporating quality control techniques.

The British Deming Association was formed in 1987 with the assistance of a number of leading UK businesses and individuals. Its principal aims are:

■ To promote a greater awareness and understanding of the importance of Dr Deming's philosophy.
■ To help people adopt the Deming approach.
■ To provide a forum for members and facilitate exchange of information.
■ To form a supportive network with links to Dr Deming's and other international authorities.

Malcolm Baldrige National Quality Award

The Baldrige Award was instituted in 1987. It is named after the US Commerce Secretary who died in 1986. The competition is managed by the National Institute of Standards and Technology. Each year two awards are given in each of the three categories, namely, manufacturing, service and small business.

To win a Baldrige Award companies have to submit an application form describing their quality practices and performance in the seven required areas. These are:

- Leadership (100)
- Information and analysis (70)
- Strategic quality planning (60)
- Human resource utilization (150)
- Quality assurance of products and services (140)
- Quality results (180)
- Customer satisfaction (300)

What are the examiners looking for under each category?

1. **Leadership**: Personal involvement of senior executives; the company's quality values and public responsibility.
2. **Information and analysis**: Scope and management of quality data and information; competitive comparisons and benchmarks and analysis of quality data and information.
3. **Strategic quality planning**: Strategic quality planning process and quality goals and plans.
4. **Human resource utilization**: How the company's human resource efforts support quality initiatives; employee involvement; quality education and training, employee recognition and performance measurement and employee well-being and morale.
5. **Quality assurance of products and services**: Design and introduction of quality products and services; process quality control; continuous improvement of processes, quality assessment, documentation; business process and support service quality and supplier quality.

6. **Quality results**: Product and service quality results; business processes, operational and support service quality results and supplier quality results which involve comparing suppliers' quality with that of competitors and with key benchmarks.
7. **Customer satisfaction**: Determining customer requirements and expectations; customer relationship management; customer service standards; commitment to customers; complaint resolution for quality improvement; determining customer satisfaction; customer satisfaction results and customer satisfaction comparison which involve comparisons with competitors.

Baldrige applicants are screened by examiners from industry and academia. Then the high scorers are visited by examiners who make recommendations to the panel of judges.

Early winners of the awards have included companies like Motorola, General Motors' Cadillac Division and Xerox. Robert Galvin, chairman of electronics group Motorola, calls the award 'the most important catalyst for transforming American business'. However, there are some people who feel, for some companies, a Baldrige Award has been a kiss of death. There are examples of companies who have won a Baldrige Award and yet were delivering very poor financial results. It has been reported that General Motors' Cadillac division won the Baldrige Award at a time when surveys showed American consumers did not rate its cars very highly. Other companies' quests for quality also did not have happy business endings.

European Quality Award

The European Quality Award (EQA) was developed by the European Foundation for Quality Management. The foundation was set up originally by fourteen leading Western European businesses in 1988. Its membership now exceeds 300 companies. In addition to providing a forum for quality issues, the foundation launched the annual European Quality Award in 1992.

The model is shown in Figure 2.4. A distinction is drawn between how the results are achieved (Enablers) and results

Total quality management

themselves (Results). There are nine criteria which are assigned a weighting and under which the assessment has to be undertaken. These are:

Enablers
- Leadership (100)
- People management (90)
- Policy and strategy (80)
- Resources (90)
- Processes (140)

Results
- People satisfaction (90)
- Customer satisfaction (200)
- Impact on society (60)
- Business results (150)

1. **Leadership**: How the executive team and all other managers inspire and drive total quality as the company's fundamental process for continuous improvement. Evidence is required of visible involvement in leading total quality, a consistent total quality culture, timely recognition and appreciation of the efforts and successes of individuals and teams, support of total quality, involvement with the customers and suppliers and active promotion of total quality outside the company.
2. **Policy and strategy**: How the company incorporates the concept of total quality in the determination, communication, implementation, review and improvement of its policy and strategy. Evidence is required of how policy and strategy are formulated on the concept of total quality in relation to relevance and comprehensiveness of information, the basis of business plans, communication and regular updating and improvement.
3. **People management**: How the company releases the full potential of its people to improve the business continuously. Evidence is required of how human resources are planned and improved, the skills and capabilities of the people and their development, agreements of targets by individuals and the teams, continuous review of performance, involvement of everyone in continuous improvement, empowering of people and effective top-down and bottom-up communication.

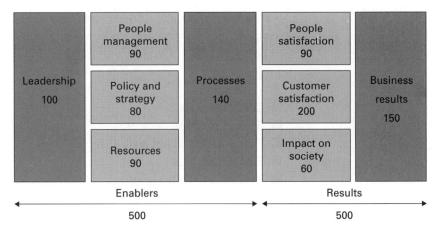

Figure 2.4 The European Quality Model. Source: European Foundation for Quality Management, EFQM Brussels Representative Office, Avenue des Pléiades 19, B-1200, Brussels, Belgium. Tel: 32 2 775 11. Fax: 32 2 775 35 35.

4. **Resources**: How the company improves its business continuously based on the concept of total quality. Evidence is required of how improvements are achieved by the management of financial, information and technological resources and by the management of suppliers, materials, buildings and equipment.

5. **Processes**: How key and support processes are identified, reviewed and, if necessary, revised to ensure continuous improvement of the company's business. Evidence is required of how processes critical to the success of business are identified, systematic management of these processes, process measurement and feedback and targets for improvements, innovation and creativity in process improvement and evaluation of benefits.

6. **Customer satisfaction**: External and internal customers' perception.

7. **People satisfaction**: What your people's feelings are about the company.

8. **Impact on society**: The community's perception of your company's performance.

9. **Business results**: What the company is achieving in relation to its planned business.

The criteria highlighted by the European Quality Award differ from the Baldrige criteria in that the European model stresses business results and focuses on businesses' impact on society.

The first European Quality Award was won by Rank Xerox in 1992. The EQA encourages organizations to take the self-assessment route and then receive feedback from independent assessors.

UK Quality Award

The UK Quality Award is managed through the British Quality Foundation and is based on the European model. The first awards were presented in November 1994 to the Rover Group and TNT Express (UK) Ltd.

ISO 9000

ISO 9000 is the international quality management systems (QMS) standard. In its present format it was introduced in 1987. It was subsequently identified by the European Commission as a vital element in the creation of the Single European Market. Many companies sought ISO 9000 registration as part of their market strategy rather than an essential part of their quality management strategy. ICL was the first company to receive group registration for ISO 9000.

According to the Lloyd's Register Quality Association and Mobil Oil research data, in 1994 the total number of European approvals was over 55 000. Significant growth was recorded in France, Italy, Germany, Austria, Norway and Portugal.

The total number of world-wide approvals at the end of 1994 was just over 70 500. Strong growth was recorded in the USA, Brazil, Japan, Taiwan, Hong Kong, South Korea and India. Progress was also made in China and Israel.

Quality management systems focus on internal processes, by installing management controls that are written down. Total quality management is concerned with developing the total organization's philosophy in relation to dealing with its customers. The two systems complement each other.

Management Ideas

Eight steps to ISO 9000

1. Evaluation of existing quality procedures against the refinements of the ISO standards.
2. Identification of corrective action needed to conform with the ISO 9000 series.
3. Preparation of a quality assurance programme.
4. Definition, documentation and implementation of new procedures.
5. Preparation of a quality manual.
6. Pre-assessment meeting with registrar to analyse quality manual.
7. Actual assessment visit.
8. Certification.

Source: Eurobusiness, January 1995, p. 71.

Does quality pay: results of LRQA survey

An interesting survey conducted by Lloyd's Register Quality Assurance (LRQA) is the market study to measure the effect of ISO 9000 on the financial and sales performance of companies in the mechanical engineering manufacturing sector. The research shows that firms registered to ISO 9000 by LRQA significantly outperformed their competitors across all the main business ratios from profitability to return on capital employed. The research, which was conducted between 1990 and 1992, at the height of the UK's recession, involved 200 companies from the mechanical engineering manufacturing sector.

The results of the LRQA survey of approved mechanical engineering manufacturing companies were:

■ Small organizations (turnover £5–10 million) have the highest profits compared to the industry average at 6.8 per cent.

■ Medium (turnover £20–50 million) and large organization (turnover in excess of £50 million) both recorded profit margins of 4 per cent, more than twice the industry average.

■ Large and small companies reported a return on capital employed (ROCE) figure of 16 and 17 per cent respectively, more than double the industry average.

■ Large organizations showed the greatest improvement with a 95 per cent increase in sales per employee over the industry average of £93 500 per employee.

■ Small and medium sized companies both recorded a profit per employee figure more than double that of the industry average.

Source: Lloyd's Register Quality Assurance Ltd, Norfolk House, Wellesley Road, Croydon, CR9 2DT.

TQM success stories in a nutshell

Rank Xerox UK Ltd

Rank Xerox UK Ltd launched a world-wide programme in 1989 called 'Leadership Through Quality'. This led to winning the Deming Prize, the Malcolm Baldrige Award and the very first European Quality Award. To Rank Xerox, TQM means the totality of quality management. The company achieved transformation by focusing attention on reward and compensation, training, communication, senior management behaviour and standards and measurement. The director of quality and communication at Rank Xerox categorized enablers of quality achievement as 'open honest communication', 'organization reflection and learning' and 'process improvement'.

TQM philosophy means that managers are expected to promote and use 'leadership through quality' tools personally. They hire and promote exponents of 'leadership through quality', seek and act on feedback, recognize and reward effective application of 'quality through leadership'. The emphasis throughout is on behaviour and performance. No wonder Rank Xerox is constantly cited as an organization that turned itself round and became more competitive through pursuing a company-wide quality programme.

ICL

At ICL the quality initiative began in 1986 and over the years it has gone through three stages, each one with a focus of its own. The director of quality and customer care presented the following explanations at a conference:

'Stage one began in 1986 with a focus on quality conformance – Do It Right First Time. At this stage 35 group quality staff were involved and detailed reporting to the headquarters was required. There was very little ownership of the initiative at line managers' level.

'At stage two the focus changed to customer care. Measures and processes were restructured to change the company culture to focus towards customers. Various senior management workshops, user groups and independent satisfaction surveys were organized to meet the objectives of delighting the customer. There was no reporting to the headquarters and the line managers experienced some ownership of the programme.

'At stage three the focus changed to self-assessment using the model of the European Quality Foundation. The progress has been fast and there is total ownership of the quality programme at all levels.'

Miliken Industrials

According to Clive Jeanes, managing director of Miliken Europe, quality is a moving target. At Miliken they have realized that the pursuit of excellence requires a constant reappraisal of what 'quality' actually means. Miliken has been working on total quality management for fifteen years. In 1980 Mr Roger Miliken went to Japan to study competitors. In February 1981, soon after he returned from Japan, Miliken had its first company-wide meeting of some 300 managers to examine how to introduce a quality improvement process. The initiative began with a narrow focus on improving the quality of the products. Subsequently, due to the influence of Tom Peters, the definition of quality was extended to incorporate customer focus. This shifted the focus from an internal to an external perspective. Miliken initiated what is now a formal, regular survey of all major customers. Then the focus moved to statistical process control to monitor and improve processes. Quality came to mean conformance to customer requirements with a minimum of variability.

Gradually over time, ideas of other 'gurus' like Schoenberger and Ishikawa were taken on board. Now quality means 'the use of all aspects of total quality to delight our customers and thus ensure our survival and long term profitable growth'.

The quality initiatives led to dramatic improvements in reducing non-conformance cost, making the right products and delivering on time. The on-time shipment performance was 77 per cent. This in 1991 went up to 99.9 per cent. Miliken has seen breakthroughs in area after area in businesses where they thought this would not have been possible.

There are numerous other success stories of companies who have achieved significant improvements as a result of adopting total quality management. The success stories act as incentives for suppliers to embark upon the total quality journey. Miliken, for example, suggested that Ciba Geigy, the Swiss chemical giant, use total quality management practices. Toyota asked Philips Electronics to improve its quality in supplying headlamps. Philips, which made light bulbs for Honda, was told that its defect rate of one faulty bulb in fifty was not good enough. Philips obliged and even exceeded Honda's requirement. Motorola helps its suppliers wade through the Baldrige applications and it even holds coaching classes.

Why total quality management fails for some companies

Various surveys conducted by Arthur D. Little of 500 American manufacturing and service companies found that only a third felt their total quality programmes were having a 'significant impact'. A. T. Kearney's survey of over 100 British firms indicated similar results.

For some companies going for quality awards has been a kiss of death. Consider the fate of company A. This company manufactures cleaning equipment. In 1993 the company decided to go through the route of total quality management in order to satisfy its customers and increase its market share.

All its 800 employees were put through the quality training programmes and the workers were divided into groups and put into work teams. Every employee was given a key ring on which was inscribed 'I am for quality'. Every two weeks a senior manager would gather all his employees and talk on different aspects of quality.

The factory floor was buzzing with quality fever. All the conversations were along the line of cycle time, service excellence and on-time delivery. The company saw its operational performance improve dramatically. However the financial results and market share analysis did not prove to be consistent with operational performance improvements.

What was happening was that the company became very inward-focused. In order to go through the hoops of the quality journey this company 'forgot' its customers. Staff were so busy improving operational procedures and delivering on time that they did not find out about their customers' needs. The company was losing sales and the costs were escalating. When the company posted a big loss after making profits before taking quality initiatives, it decided to get rid of 200 employees and abandoned the quality initiative.

There are many examples of other companies like company A who have gone through considerable efforts to become quality-driven companies and ended with failures.

Why do well-intentioned companies do not find success in quality?

These are some of the reasons which were highlighted in various studies, reports and surveys:

- Failure of management to set realistic goals or look for measurable benefits at the outset.
- Objectives set have not been sensible and there were no time limits.
- TQM was embarked upon to impress customers and suppliers but the company itself had no conviction.
- There has been no focus on customers but only on processes.
- Quality was treated as an operational issue and delegated to the quality department.
- The company set up a bureaucratic system to achieve quality goals.
- TQM was treated as a 'quick fix'.
- A powerful set of company values was lacking.
- Staff were not adequately trained.
- Some companies introduced TQM as an excuse for downsizing.
- TQM was not aligned to corporate strategy
- The company lacked strong leadership.
- Employees were not empowered.
- Teams were formed without giving serious thought as to their structure and objectives.
- TQM was instituted to win awards.
- Some companies introduced TQM without monitoring costs.
- Lack of support from employees, especially where morale is undermined by redundancies.
- Lack of integration with strategic objectives.
- The company had adopted wrong strategic choices.
- Many companies did not apply bottom-line discipline to quality.
- To some companies standards became more important than sales.

42

How not to fail

1. Total quality management is both a philosophy and a way of doing business in the 1990s. Organizations have to reflect about what, how and why they do what they do and they have to take appropriate actions continuously in order to listen to their customers and consequently improve their business performance.

2. Companies like Rank Xerox, ICL, Motorola, Miliken, Philips Electronics, Rover Group, TNT, Design to Distribution (D2D), the ICL subsidiary, have worked with TQM for a very long time in order to become 'quality companies'. Quality to these companies is not a destination but a journey. The quality programme has to be constantly monitored and changed as the competitive scenario changes.

3. The top management should make themselves personally responsible for quality and gain commitment and involvement from their staff. There should be a commitment and conviction throughout the organization. The quest for quality depends on an employee's conviction and commitment and his or her behaviour towards his colleagues and customers as driven by the organization's mission and vision.

    The author recently was speaking to two employees from a pharmaceutical company who were celebrating the end of a quality project. They said they have been working on the project for nearly three years. The project is now finished and they went on to say 'Thank God, we can get back to our proper work'. Where does the blame lie?

4. For total quality management to be successful the **philosophy** must be prevention not detection, **commitment** and **involvement** of all staff must be 100 per cent, the **approach** must be senior management-led, the **scope** must be company-wide, the **scale** must be everyone in the company as well as suppliers and distributors, the **control** must be cost, the **theme** must be continuous improvement, and the **focus** must be customer satisfaction.

5. In management a distinction is made between an efficient organization and an effective organization. Efficiency is doing the right thing whereas effectiveness is doing 'the

right thing right'. In relation to Figure 2.5 the quality company should aim to occupy the segment marked 'A'. To do 'the right thing right' in TQM means that a company should avoid all those failure factors highlighted in this chapter and set a vision that will put 'fire in their employees' bellies'.

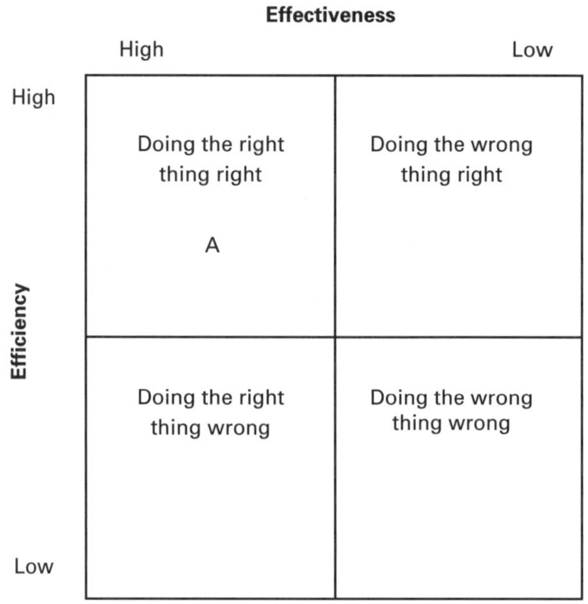

Effectiveness

	High	Low
High	Doing the right thing right A	Doing the wrong thing right
Low	Doing the right thing wrong	Doing the wrong thing wrong

(Efficiency)

Figure 2.5 Efficiency versus effectiveness

Quality in the European Union

According to the EC Directorate, manufacturers and distributors throughout the European Union will in the future have to make sure that their products meet the requirements of the appropriate directive and conform to standards by displaying the CE Mark. Failure to comply and display the CE Mark is a legal offence and will lead to prosecution. Some directives are already in force while others are imminent.

Quality soundbites of 1990s

- Good quality does not necessarily mean high quality.
- Quality means delighting the customer.
- Quality is a philosophy of business.
- Quality is not a destination but a journey.
- Love to learn quality.
- Quality management is a source of profit.
- Quality is everybody's business.
- Quality differentiates companies from the competition.
- The only way you are going to retain your business is to deliver 100 per cent quality.
- A quality company lives for its customers.
- The key to quality success is to focus total commitment outside the individual to within.
- Total quality management is implemented by many organizations out of desperation rather than inspiration.
- Customers measure quality to competition not to specifications. Ignoring quality in the 1990s is tantamount to corporate suicide.
- Total quality should be a core part of everyone's job description.
- Training for quality is not a programme – it is a process.
- Quality is like a religion; you have to have faith in it.
- Total quality is synonymous with the strategic plan of a business.
- Quality is excellence in execution.
- Total quality unlocks people potential.
- Total quality creates a commitment by the company to its employees. Total quality brings an end to 'either/or' thinking.
- Total quality philosophy challenges conventional Western management.
- Total quality creates high-performing organizations.
- Total quality enables organizations to out-think their competitors.
- Quality should be considered as a marathon not as a 100-metre race.
- Total quality requires sustainable commitment.
- The foremost requirement of TQM is to get people to internalize and own the initiative.

Is your organization a quality organization? Find out for yourself

Scoring: Score 1 for 'Yes', 2 for 'Yes but...' and 3 for 'No'.

1. Our company's mission statement explicitly mentions quality and customer service.   Yes/Yes but.../No
2. Our strategic plan includes a strategy for quality.   Yes/Yes but.../No
3. Our chief executive officer himself or herself gets involved with quality.   Yes/Yes but.../No
4. Senior managers in our company regularly visit our customers.   Yes/Yes but.../No
5. All levels of management in our organization get training on quality and customer service.   Yes/Yes but.../No
6. We regularly conduct customer surveys.   Yes/Yes but.../No
7. We believe in product quality and service quality.   Yes/Yes but.../No
8. We treat everyone outside as well as inside the organization as our customers.   Yes/Yes but.../No
9. All departments and divisions are concerned about quality.   Yes/Yes but.../No
10. Quality is an investment not a cost.   Yes/Yes but.../No
11. We are allowed to make mistakes as long as we learn from them.   Yes/Yes but.../No
12. Quality is a never ending process.   Yes/Yes but.../No
13. Our appraisal system incorporates assessing our behaviour towards our customers and colleagues.   Yes/Yes but.../No
14. We benchmark our competitors.   Yes/Yes but.../No
15. We communicate freely and honestly within our company.   Yes/Yes but.../No
16. We have a flat organization.   Yes/Yes but.../No
17. We get recognition for our efforts in the company's performance.   Yes/Yes but.../No
18. Quality in our company is everybody's business.   Yes/Yes but.../No
19. We work with our suppliers and distributors as partners.   Yes/Yes but.../No
20. Employees are empowered in our company.   Yes/Yes but.../No

Score: 20   You are definitely working in a top quality company.

       21–30 Your company is almost a quality company.

       31–40 Your company should make an extra effort to become a quality company.

       41–50 You are heading towards extinction unless you embark upon a quality initiative.

       51–60 Your company is a dinosaur. Its days are numbered.

Quality and trust

The quest for quality depends on the inner feelings of employees. How employees feel about their job, about their organization and about their bosses' influences on their behaviour in delivering total quality. Organizations which have won quality awards have to sustain their standards over a very long period and the sustainability depends on employees' conviction in what they do, and their commitment. They have to trust their organizations in recognizing their efforts, and it is the trust within the organization that motivates them and that drives them to achieve business excellence. Without such trust organizations can spend millions of dollars on consultants and on grand quality projects and win awards but very soon they will lose out.

Selected reading

Business Week (1991) The Quality Imperative. December 2.
Business Week (1994) Making Quality Pay. August 8.
Philip B. Crosby (1989) *Let's Talk Quality*. McGraw-Hill.
The Economist Intelligence Unit (1992) *Making Quality Work*.
John Macdonald and John Piggot. (1990) *Global Quality*. Mercury.
The Open University Business School, Course B889, Unit 7.

3 Benchmarking

in brief "Mirror, mirror on the wall, who is the prettiest of them all?"

Summary

■ To compete companies now copy other companies' best practice. This practice is called benchmarking.
■ Benchmarking is a method used to improve business performance in order to adopt best practice.
■ Xerox are recognized as an originator of benchmarking practice.
■ Benchmarking is practised by many companies including Rank Xerox, AT&T, Motorola, Miliken, Ford and Federal Express.
■ Benchmarking is now used across all functions.
■ The practice has become the cornerstone of total quality management, business process re-engineering and time-based management.
■ Step-by-step guidelines are provided in conducting benchmarking.
■ How to use quality models as a framework for benchmarking.
■ How to incorporate 'the voice of the customer' by benchmarking.
■ How benchmarking has been conducted in practice. Case studies: Royal Mail, Thomson Travel Group and Rover.
■ Troubleshooting guidelines.
■ Sources of information.
■ Benchmarking as a means to an end.

Copycat era

Over the past few years benchmarking has become very popular in many organizations. Achieving sustainable levels of growth and profitability has become increasingly difficult for many organizations as competitive pressures are intensifying. To improve organizational performance and effectiveness, businesses over the past few years have embarked upon benchmarking in the areas of manufacturing operations, marketing and customer service. Recently the practice has been extended to other functions such as finance and people management.

What is benchmarking?

Benchmarking is a method of improving business performance by learning from other companies how to do things better in order to be the 'best in the class'. Rank Xerox defines benchmarking as:

> A continuous systematic process of evaluating companies recognized as industry leaders, to determine business and work processes that represent 'best practice' and establish rational performance goals.

Other organizations define the practice as:

> The on-going and objective measurement. . .of relative performance. . .against relevant organizations. . .in key process areas.

> A change programme which enables the achievement of the 'best practice'.

At IBM benchmarking is 'the continuous process of analysing the best practice in the world for the process goals and objectives leading to world class levels of achievement'.

It does not matter which definition we look at, all of them emphasize the fact that the benchmarking practice should be **continuous**, **systematic** and it should involve **evaluation** and **measurement** with a view to achieving excellence and becoming the 'best in class'. Benchmarking is the cornerstone of total quality management.

Management Ideas

To quote John McClelland, European director of manufacturing and product development, IBM UK Ltd, the main objectives of benchmarking at IBM are:

- 'To ensure that our business process goals are set to exceed the best qualitative results achieved by world class leaders.
- To incorporate best practice throughout IBM business processes.
- To reach a level of maturity where benchmarking is an ongoing part of the management system in all areas of the business.'

Benchmarking originated in the USA approximately a decade ago. Now 95 per cent of US companies say they are practising it. In the late 1970s Xerox, who are recognized as being the originator of benchmarking, found that the retail price of Canon photocopiers was lower than Xerox's manufacturing costs. They a sent a benchmarking team to Japan to compare their performance in a wide range of areas with their Japanese counterparts and returned to undertake the 'step change' needed to catch up. Benchmarking thus developed in Xerox in 1979 and it became a company-wide effort in 1981.

Benchmarking in Europe

As far as Europe is concerned, benchmarking seems to be well established. Coopers & Lybrand undertook a survey in 1994 covering *The Times* 1000 companies or their equivalent across five European countries: the United Kingdom, the Netherlands, Switzerland, Spain and France. The survey defined benchmarking as 'the process of comparing business practices and performance levels between companies (or divisions within companies) in order to gain new insights and to identify opportunities for making improvements.'

The survey showed that over two-thirds of companies in the United Kingdom, the Netherlands and Switzerland, over half of French companies and a third of Spanish companies are using benchmarking techniques. Benchmarking is used across all of the principal business functions.

In Japan benchmarking has been practised for a long time. Although the term benchmarking was not used, Japanese firms were conducting benchmarking exercises in the leading companies.

Early experience of benchmarking was in the manufacturing sector because manufacturing output is tangible and measured (what gets measured gets done). Gradually the techniques came to be applied to processes, logistics, financial performance, research and development and so on.

Pioneering company

Rank Xerox, in its quest to become an excellent company, benchmarked against different companies in various operational areas (see Table 3.1). This is a classic example of benchmarking outside the direct competitor set.

A benchmarking analysis can be conducted for any type of organization covering a wide range of functional areas. They can be commercial or not-for-profit organizations. Functional areas include manufacturing, finance, marketing, health and safety, personnel and so on.

These days various organizations are forming strategic alliances and partnerships which give them an opportunity to benchmark with their partners. In the early 1990s, the Rover Group started a benchmarking programme. They benchmarked against Honda with whom they had a collaborative relationship. Rover Body and Pressings was chosen to pilot the benchmarking process within the Rover Group.

In some cases, benchmarking developed from conducting competitor analysis. This was the case for Royal Doulton who

Table 3.1 Benchmarking by Rank Xerox

Companies benchmarked against	*Areas benchmarked against*
Miliken	Employee suggestions
Toyota, Fuji, Xerox	Total quality management
AT&T, Hewlett Packard	R&D
Proctor & Gamble	Product marketing
LL Bean, Hershey Foods	Logistics
American Hospital Supply	Inventory control
American Express	Billing and collection

took its first steps towards benchmarking in 1987. Royal Doulton undertook competitor analysis with Wedgwood in the UK, Rosenthal, Hutschenreuther and Villeroy & Boch in Germany, Noritake in Japan and Lenox in the USA. The benchmarking exercise that was undertaken subsequently led to technical and process best practice.

Benchmarking is embedded into various approaches to organizational development and improvement. It is the cornerstone of the total quality management, business process re-engineering and time-based management.

What are the advantages of benchmarking?

First of all, benchmarking can only happen in a culture in which people are prepared to have their thinking challenged and are prepared to learn from one another.

The practice offers the following advantages:

- Provides direction and impetus for improvement.
- Indicates early warning of competitive disadvantage.
- Promotes competitive awareness.
- Becomes the stepping stones to 'breakthrough' thinking.
- Identifies the 'best practice'.
- Provides an objective attainment standard for key areas of business operations.
- Links operational tactics to corporate vision and strategy.
- Exposes performance gaps.
- Triggers major step changes in business performance.
- Helps companies redefine their objectives.
- Challenges the 'status quo'.
- Allows realistic stretch goals.

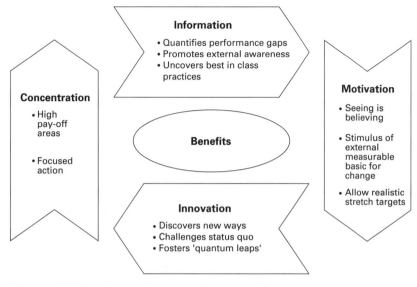

Figure 3.1 The different benefits of benchmarking

Benchmarking at work

Table 3.2 is an example of benchmarking at work which appeared in *Business Week*, 7 December 1992.

Table 3.2 Benchmarking at work: improving procurement

	Typical company	World-class company
Cost factors		
Suppliers per purchasing agent	34	5
Agents per $100m of purchase	5.4	2.2
Purchasing costs as a % of purchase made	3.3%	0.8%
Time factors		
Supplier evaluations (weeks)	3	0.4
Supplier lead times (weeks)	150	8
Time spent placing an order (weeks)	6	0.001
Quality of deliveries		
Late	33%	2%
Rejected	1.5%	0.0001%
Materials shortage (no. of instances per year)	400	4

Data: McKinsey & Co.

How to benchmark

Rank Xerox proposes ten steps to benchmarking under the categories of Planning, Analysis and Integration.

Planning   Step 1   Identify subject to benchmark.
Step 2   Identify the best practice.
Step 3   Collect data.

Analysis   Step 4   Analyse-determine current competitive gaps.
Step 5   Project future performance.

Integration   Step 6   Communicate results and analysis.
Step 7   Establish goals.
Step 8   Develop action plan
Step 9   Implement plan and monitor results.
Step 10   Recalibrate the benchmark

Source: The Economist Conferences. 'Benchmarking' conference

Step 1

Assuming that organization A is intending to benchmark. First of all A should identify the subject to benchmark. It could be corporate vision, or specific function or process or the attributes of a specific product. Let us assume that A has identified customer service as the subject for benchmarking.

Customer service can be defined in the operating terms of quality and delivery performance. A customer-driven operating system impacts the measurement of workflow from department to department.

Step 2

Identify the best practice in the customer service area. What constitutes best practice in this area and how would one measure it?

One could look at customer ratings from surveys, number of complaints received, revenue per customer, retention rate, repeat business, lapse rate, on-time delivery, delivery of defect-free products, etc. The best practice in customer service is identified, let us say, in company B. Company A will choose company B as its benchmarking candidate.

54

Step 3

This stage involves gathering data on various criteria chosen. For example, if company B is a parcel delivery service then step 3 would involve collecting information on parcel delivery services.

Step 4

This step involves analysing data collected and comparing the level and quality of service to that provided by company A. This stage would determine performance or competitive gaps in providing customer service.

Different companies use combinations of methods to find out the level of customer service they provide. IBM, for example, during the design of AS/400 mini-computer, solicited users' opinions on the product and brought software companies into the planning process.

Other ways of 'staying close to your customers' involve visiting customers, conducting surveys, and instituting quality functional development as done by Hewlett-Packard and the Ford Motor Company. As has already been explained, quality function deployment is a system of designing a product or service which integrates marketing, design and manufacturing functions. This method involves all 'specialists' right from the beginning when the product is conceived.

Step 5

This level would demand formulation of the project to close the competitive gaps and to set benchmarks towards achieving best practice.

Step 6

Etc.

This stage involves communicating the objectives of the project to all those involved in effecting improvements. Communication at this stage is crucial to set the direction of the project. The subsequent steps lead to formulating strategy (**What you want to do**), setting time scale (**when you** want to finish the project), preparing an action plan (**how and who should do it**) and setting benchmarks for implementation. Finally the best practice project is implemented and regularly monitored. The Deming cycle (plan, do, act, review) mentioned in Chapter 2 should come into play.

Benchmarking can also be done with reference to the value chain. A comparison can be made for each stage of the value chain. Benchmarking can be undertaken in relation to 'inbound logistics', 'outbound logistics', and so on.

What aspects of business to benchmark?

In general all aspects of business operations can be benchmarked. In achieving organizational transformation all aspects of business should be benchmarked. However in order to prioritize it is recommended that consideration be given to the shareholders' as well customers' values (see Figure 3.2). The High-High box should be the first candidate for benchmarking where it is not possible to undertake benchmarking for all aspects of business.

Figure 3.2 Aspects of business to benchmark

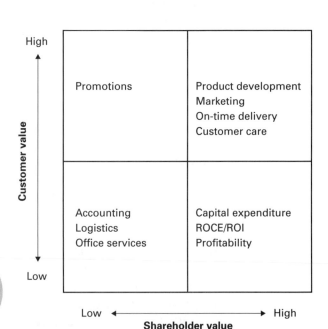

The European Quality Model and benchmarking

The European Quality Model can be used to provide a structure to benchmarking. If we take 'Enablers' then each part can be taken to benchmark against 'partners'.

Enablers

■ **Leadership**: In this aspect benchmarking can be done to find the involvement of top management in any change project; if employees get due recognition for their efforts and, if so, what type of recognition? What type of leadership is practised in a partner's organization; is top management involved with customers, suppliers and distributors directly?

■ **Policy and strategy**: How is corporate strategy formulated; the content of the mission statement; the inclusion of employees' and customers' needs in the mission statement; the way objectives are formulated and communicated across the organization; the use of a control cycle and regular review.

■ **People management**: Formation of self-performing teams; extent of empowerment; development of competences and training; employees' needs analysis; employees' development and advancement; employees' appraisal and the subsequent actions.

■ **Resources**: How are people enabled to perform their tasks; availability of appropriate financial and non-financial resources; use, type and level of technology.

■ **Processes**: Identifying key processes; activities connected with key processes; how are key processes monitored and reviewed; how is creativity and innovation encouraged; methods of process improvement.

Types of benchmarking

There are different types of benchmarking depending on whether the benchmarking is conducted with an external organization or within the organization itself. Then there are benchmarking practices which relate to products, processes, people and different functions.

Competitive benchmarking

When Xerox sent a team of manufacturing people to Japan to study processes, products and material, the objective was to gain a benchmark that could be used by Xerox to measure against Canon their competitor. This is an example of competitive benchmarking.

The best example of competitive benchmarking that was used to achieve a quantum leap is given by Michael Hammer in his book *Re-engineering the Corporation* in which he gives an example of the Ford Motor Company's efforts to improve its account payable operations. Ford benchmarked against Mazda and ended up removing its non-value added activities and thus achieving a reduction in headcount from 500 people to five people. This story is told by everyone at every benchmarking and process re-engineering conference.

Strategic benchmarking

PIMS (the profit impact of marketing strategy) defines strategic benchmarking as the development of measures for a business unit which quantifies its key strengths and weaknesses, to give some external reference to the strategic planning process. In an article entitled 'Strategic benchmarking at ICI Fibres', Clayton and Luchs cite the example of how ICI Fibres, when faced with crisis in 1980, undertook an extensive competitive analysis of the European market. The strategic problem facing ICI Fibres was in the area of quality and productivity in its polyester position. Analysis of the strengths and weaknesses of competitors ICI had to face was undertaken in each fibre area. The factors influencing the long term profitability were reviewed and ICI came to the conclusion that its share positions in most of the nylon businesses were still strong and its quality in textile fibres was good enough to justify a price promotion. Evaluation of sustainable earning power from strategic benchmark comparisons showed a clearer picture of the future earning potential. Strategic benchmarking, therefore, aims at strategic changes and prioritized resource allocation.

Process benchmarking

Organizations can compare internal processes between countries or companies or divisions within the same group. They can compare their own processes with industry leading service providers.

Sears plc benchmarked the retail supply chain, focusing attention on core delivery processes which develop, select and deliver products to the customer. They looked at range, design, source, price, distribution, display and sales, all these constituting components of supply chain management. Externally they benchmarked against Xerox, Wallmart, Nestle, ICL, Marks & Spencer and British Airways.

Florida Power and Lights (FPL) in pursuit of a Deming Award benchmarked with Kansai Electric of Japan. They benchmarked the process of repairing boiler tube leaks.

Product benchmarking

In the 1970s IBM issued instructions that all new products must have a superior performance to both their IBM precursor and the best of their competitors' products from the moment of the very first customer shipment. Thus, product benchmarking was born throughout the corporation. Products were benchmarked on the basis of functionality, reliability and availability.

Product benchmarking is the most widespread form of benchmarking in Japan. This is due to the 'me too' mentality of Japanese firms.

Benchmarking customer service

Customer service is a complex supply chain of service to customers. Benchmarking in this field will identify where performance is below expectation and where there is room for improvement compared with competitors.

Some organizations, like ICL, started benchmarking customer service first by defining customer needs and then by using customer satisfaction surveys to identify the level of service being provided. The next stage was to compare the service level with the customer requirement. By matching customer needs with the level of service delivered and by using service delivery costs from the benchmarking surveys, the appropriate action was taken to implement change and deliver excellence.

Internal benchmarking

Some organizations undertake internal benchmarking in order to improve existing performance and also as a first step towards external benchmarking.

Taking Sears plc as an example again, the company is a grouping of autonomous businesses with varied backgrounds and culture. These businesses are represented by Selfridges, Saxone, Freeman Hardy and Willis, Olympus, Adams and others. They have focused their attention on operations, sourcing, in-store presentation, supply chain and service in order to deliver retail brand and image.

Pitney Bowes has carried out a number of internal benchmarking exercises over two years focusing attention on new product introduction, order fulfilment, customer satisfaction and purchasing.

Internal benchmarking is undertaken to compare similar operations or functions across the company or group. For example, if you were to take the Economist Group, the internal benchmaking would be conducted between the Economist Newspapers Ltd and the Economist Intelligence Unit in relation to a specific service or process, e.g. order fulfilment.

Some authors recommend doing internal benchmarking for the following reasons:

- To establish an internal baseline.
- To identify performance gaps in various activities.
- To identify areas that need improving.
- To establish common practice and procedures.
- To bring about effective communication process within the organization.
- To promote an understanding of the nature of benchmarking.
- To instil confidence in undertaking external benchmarking.

The gap between internal and external practice has provided change champions with powerful evidence with which to overcome internal resistance to change.

Benchmarking, quality and the voice of the customers

Benchmarking is an integral part of the total quality management initiative. Let us assume that an ice cream company called Delight wants to compare its product in relation to its competitor, another ice cream company called Heaven. Delight can use the quality deployment function to match the attributes of its product and its competitor's product in relation to customers' needs (Figure 3.3).

Delight can then benchmark its products' attributes against the attributes of its competitor's product (Figure 3.4). Based on the findings, Delight can make the best ice cream and gain competitive advantage over Heaven.

Figure 3.3 Quality function deployment – ice cream

Product attributes

Consumer needs	Taste	Colour	Texture	Flavour	Hard/ soft
Taste	8				
Colour		8			
Texture			7		
Flavour				4	
Hard					1 Soft

Figure 3.4 Benchmarking – Delight versus Heaven

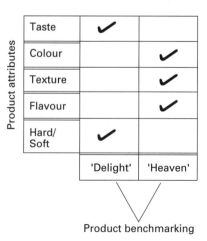

Product attributes

	'Delight'	'Heaven'
Taste	✔	
Colour		✔
Texture		✔
Flavour		✔
Hard/ Soft	✔	

Product benchmarking

Benchmarking without emotions

Avon Products Inc. is the world's leading seller and marketer of beauty related goods. The annual turnover in 1994 was in excess of $3.5 billion and it markets its products in more than 100 countries through 1.5 million independent representatives. Avon is also the world's largest manufacturer of fashion jewellery. The trigger point for them was to review their business with the customers. They used a service quality survey method called 'servqual' which measured customer expectations and perceptions from which they identified performance gaps.

They grouped together into regional teams in order to identify 'best practice'. The benchmarking was done against the 'ideal service unit' which enabled everyone to work towards a goal without the emotions of feeling unfairly compared.

Benchmarking methods can now be viewed as falling into three broad categories depending on whether the focus is on metrics, processes or the strategy, structures and culture of the organization. Within each category, a different type of benchmarking can be used to diagnose a problem or assess a performance gap, or help redesign process or strategy to help implement a new change programme. The types are illustrated in Figure 3.5.

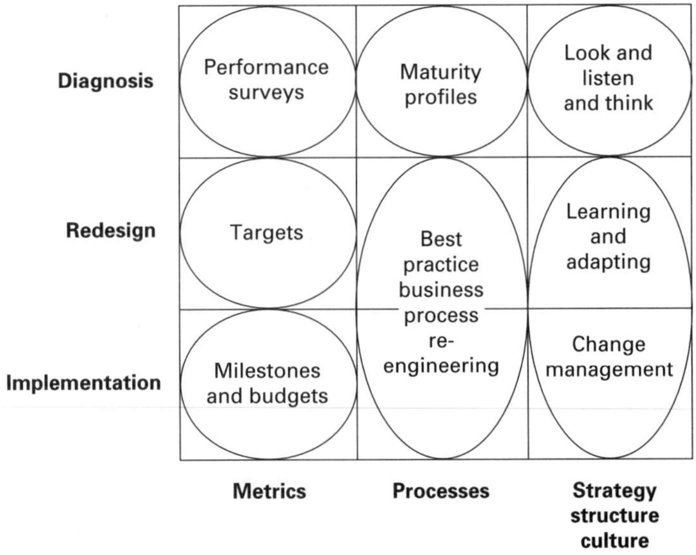

Figure 3.5 Types of benchmarking

	Metrics	Processes	Strategy structure culture
Diagnosis	Performance surveys	Maturity profiles	Look and listen and think
Redesign	Targets	Best practice business process re-engineering	Learning and adapting
Implementation	Milestones and budgets		Change management

Benchmarking case studies

Case study 1: Royal Mail

Royal Mail sees best practice benchmarking (BPB) as a valuable tool in achieving its declared mission to be recognized as the world's best distributor of text and packages.

The quality department developed materials to help benchmark teams, based on the flowchart in Figure 3.6. The same process can be followed for any benchmarking activity.

Figure 3.6
Benchmarking: a strategic approach.
© Royal Mail 1990

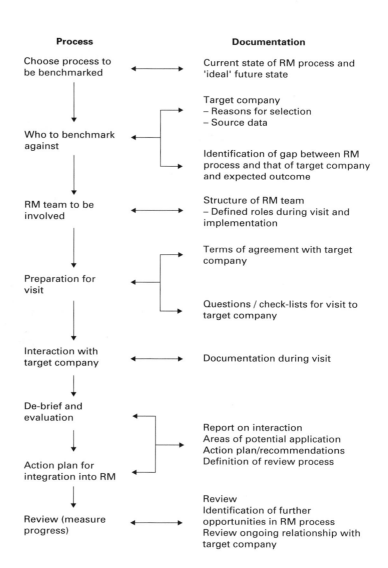

Process	Documentation
Choose process to be benchmarked	Current state of RM process and 'ideal' future state
Who to benchmark against	Target company – Reasons for selection – Source data Identification of gap between RM process and that of target company and expected outcome
RM team to be involved	Structure of RM team – Defined roles during visit and implementation
Preparation for visit	Terms of agreement with target company Questions / check-lists for visit to target company
Interaction with target company	Documentation during visit
De-brief and evaluation	Report on interaction Areas of potential application Action plan/recommendations Definition of review process
Action plan for integration into RM	
Review (measure progress)	Review Identification of further opportunities in RM process Review ongoing relationship with target company

Management Ideas

This clarity in defining how the benchmarking process works has helped communicate the value of it and involve all staff in implementing it. An example of how the awareness of benchmarking has cascaded throughout the culture can be seen in a benchmarking exercise recently started within the marketing department. Brought together at a departmental conference, a team of benchmarking volunteers is working through the process defined by the flowchart. The team, which is given special training, is made up of a mixture of functions within the marketing department, giving a variety of perspectives.

The team decided to focus on aspects of product development, including the management of consultants and internal communications. It found that the best practice in product development transfers easily between industries, opening up the opportunity for a wide spread of benchmarking partners. One over-riding criterion it imposed in selecting partners was that they should share a total quality focus.

Case study 2: Thomson Travel Group

Thomson have been a market leader in tour operations for over twenty years. In his presentation at the HR Benchmarking conference organized by the Economist Conferences, Martin Brackenbury of Thomson Travel Group said, 'We continuously track our competitors on a number of indicators. In our competitor comparisons, we track more than thirty key indicators and maintain our leadership in more than 95 per cent of them.

But it is not sufficient for us to benchmark within our industry, as well as considering our competitors' performance, we need to look world-wide to identify who, anywhere, in any service industry, is doing anything exceptionally well, and to identify what we can learn from them to add to our own competitiveness.

We arranged a benchmark tour to the US and within a week we visited ten organizations, from different industry sectors with one thing in common: a reputation for excellence in customer service. The companies visited were:

Hampton Inn	Low cost hotels
Stew Leonard's	Supermarkets
Paul Rever	Disability insurance

Benchmarking

Fidelity	Financial services
Ritz-Carlton	De luxe hotels
Polaroid	Cameras and film
Nordstrom	Department stores
Southwest	No frills airline
TGI Friday	Theme restaurants
Sewell Village Cadillac	Car dealer and maintenance
Home Depot	DIY warehouse stores
Super Shuttle	Airport transfers

What did we learn?

- You have to focus on key aspects of the organization only.
- We discovered, when comparing ourselves with the very best, that we have a lot to learn. While we may be better than our competitors we are a lot less good than the best.
- Benchmarking is exhilarating. Despite the fact that, as our tour progressed, we discovered that, measure for measure, we had more to learn than to teach, we were exhilarated by what we had seen because we knew that there was much that we could apply.
- It was confirmed that customers set their expectations of service from your industry in relation to their experience of excellent service from other industries.
- Measuring a range of different companies changes your outlook and understanding of what is excellent.
- Excellence is achieved through people at all levels with the right attitudes, knowledge and skills, and all distinctive performing companies have distinctive HR practices.
- We learnt more about:

  - the mechanics of empowerment
  - hiring the right people
  - fun and recognition
  - communication
  - selection
  - incentivization. . .'

Case study 3: Rover Group

The following is an extract from the case study which appeared in *UK Quality*, March 1995. Mr John Towers is a group chief executive.

Management Ideas

Learning from Honda

Rover took a long time to recognize why Japanese cars were more successful, but a visit by senior staff to Honda's North American plant in Ohio precipitated an attitudinal breakthrough. Though executives had visited Japan earlier, the US visit enabled them to see Japanese best practice in a Western context. The realization, as Mr Towers puts it, that 'we couldn't just copy Japanese techniques but we had to observe the benefit of what was being done and why, then determine ways in which we could apply it to our business' led to the Rover 'Working with Pride' initiative and the start in 1987 of the total quality improvement (TQI) programme.

Rover's breakthrough came when it recognized that culture plays only a small part in Japanese business success. 'In fact, the Japanese philosophy for success is extremely straightforward', Mr Towers says. 'Get the design of the products and processes right to the smallest detail, empower your employees to run and continually improve those processes, and profits will naturally flow.'

From Honda, Rover learned the 'new model centre' concept. 'This was an example of our new diligence, using a people-centred philosophy,' Mr Towers says. First used on the Rover 200 series, the objective is to produce a world class fit and finish through continuous process validation. A small flexible core planning team works on the product from concept through the various stages of design and development. When pilot cars are built for product engineering (using parts provided by their ultimate suppliers) a launch team is formed that includes manufacturing and engineering staff who eventually take production management positions to ensure continuity. Supply centres are set up to support the launch team, buy components and take responsibility for controlling quality.'

Benchmarking – troubleshooting

Like any process problems do arise in practice. Table 3.3 helps troubleshooting in undertaking the benchmarking process.

Table 3.3

Problem	Likely causes	Solution
Benchmarking the wrong measure.	Inadequate knowledge of own organization and operation.	Further research to find significant measure.
Benchmarking the wrong organization.	Inadequate desk research.	More detailed initial research.
Benchmarking not leading to action.	Senior management not involved.	Ensure that management is seen to be in support.
Failure to sell idea to senior management.	Lack of information, poor presentation.	Tie benchmarking firmly to the existing business plan; show how other companies have benefited.
Lack of resources for benchmarking.	Lack of management support; exclusive ownership by the benchmarking team.	Lobby and promote benchmarking as a company-wide approach.
Data not meaningful.	Too much/too little data; data not comparable.	Tighter focus to measure and test the assumption about your processes that generated the measures.
Inaccurate/false data.	Over-reliance on public or competitor sources.	Double-check sources through personal checks.
Failure to sell idea to target organizations.	Scepticism and protective instincts.	Make clear the benefit of shared information; reassess criteria for selection of partners.
Over-reliance on superficial similarity.	Lack of rigorous criteria for assessing partners.	Re-define search to find closer fits.
Benchmark partner unwilling to share useful data.	Benchmark partner too alike.	Define search by process not industry.
Benchmark too many measures.	Unclear priorities.	Relate benchmarking to business plan.

Source: *Best Practice Benchmarking*. Management and Technology Divison, Department of Trade and Industry.

Buying into benchmarking

Benchmarking is rapidly becoming acknowledged as one of the most powerful business improvement techniques in the competitive armoury. Benchmarking centres and clubs have been formed and are being formed to enable organizations to find out how one should organize and manage benchmarking practices and how to choose benchmarking

Management Ideas

'partners'. Just as quality caught the imagination during the 1970s and 1980s, benchmarking 'clubs' are proving to be an international success in a variety of industrial sectors.

Sources of information

Information about other companies and organizations can be obtained from various sources. Highlighted below are some sources of information:

- Annual reports.
- Press material.
- Analysts' reports.
- Market research reports.
- Trade associations
- Academic case studies.
- Books.
- Competitor advertising.
- Benchmarking clubs.
- Benchmarking partners.
- Joint-venture partners.
- Government reports.
- Site visits.
- Conferences.
- Consumer surveys.
- Trade surveys.
- Media surveys.
- Retail audits.
- Salespeople.
- Product comparisons.
- Distributors and suppliers.

The Coopers & Lybrand survey (1994) shows that companies prefer to receive data from competitors, internal departments, customers and use published external data (Figure 3.7).

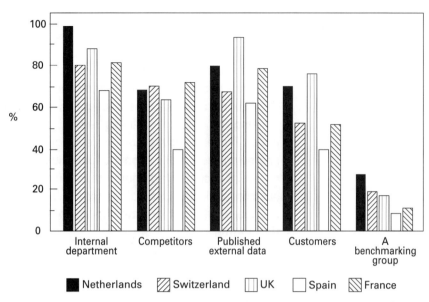

Figure 3.7 Preferred sources of data. *Source*: © Coopers & Lybrand survey 1994

The bottom line of benchmarking

Although any operation or process is open to analysis and improvement through benchmarking, without strategic direction, the approach may not have a significant impact on the organization's overall competitive position and profitability.

Identifying industry's 'best practice' is a powerful focus for change. The gap between internal and external practice can provide a starting point to overcoming resistance to change.

Research has shown that satisfied customers will tell an average of five others about their experience, but dissatisfied customers will tell an average of ten others. It is also said that quality of service is never an accident, it is the result of intelligent efforts! Benchmarking helps identify the nature of the effort made to bring about customer satisfaction or even delight.

Benchmarking as a means to an end

Most change programmes have not 'delivered the goods' so to speak because they are treated as ends in themselves. Change initiatives such as total quality management, benchmarking, process or business re-engineering are means to ends. These initiatives are not 'solutions' but are means of improving the organization's capabilities and overall performance. Benchmarking, therefore, should be undertaken with specific goals in mind rather than just bringing about any change. **It is what organizations do after benchmarking that matters**.

Selected reading

Business Week (1992) Beg, Borrow – And Benchmark. December 7.

Coopers & Lybrand (1994) *Survey of Benchmarking In Europe*. London.

Department of Trade and Industry. *Best Practice Benchmarking*.

The Economist Intelligence Unit Report. *Best Practices: Management*.

European Foundation for Quality Management. A Feedback Report on Benchmarking the Use of Self Assessment by Seven Member Companies.

Management Review (1995) Benchmarking: People make the Process. *The American Management Association Magazine*, June.

Various papers presented by IBM, ICL, Rank Xerox and Miliken at the Benchmarking conference organized by the Economist Conferences.

4

Delivering service excellence

in brief

"The kind of world one carries in oneself is the important thing, and the world outside takes all the graces, colour and value from that."

James Russell Lowell

Summary

■ Customer service became the focus and the slogan for many organizations in the 1980s and 1990s.

■ It is not what is produced that matters but how it is delivered.

■ What customers perceive, they must receive.

■ In the 1980s, organizations like ABB and Avis made customer satisfaction a part of their corporate strategy.

■ What Peter Drucker and Tom Peters have to say on customer satisfaction.

■ Many researchers show that the key drivers of corporate strategic direction are customer satisfaction, quality leadership and innovation.

■ Listening to the customer or getting close to the customer involves forming customer focus groups, visits to customers,

conducting surveys and research and providing training on customer care.
■ Customer satisfaction is one of the core components of various quality models.
■ Customer service at DHL: a case study.
■ Why some companies fail to deliver service excellence.
■ Winning the hearts and minds of employees.
■ Use of transactional analysis in providing service excellence.

Focus on customers

In the 1980s many organizations found it very hard to compete in spite of the fact that they invested heavily in numerous quality systems and projects. And the many quality projects which were to be their saviours did not help. We have already highlighted several reasons why, for some companies, quality management did not deliver what it promised to deliver. One of the key reasons for failure was lack of attention and consideration to customers.

Customers became the focus in the late 1980s and 1990s. Those organizations who paid attention to customers succeeded. The slogan was not just to satisfy the customers but to delight them. Many books, articles and research reports took on board the theme of delivering service excellence.

Forum Corporation research uncovered that almost 70 per cent of the identifiable reasons why customers left typical companies had nothing to do with the product. In 1988 it surveyed the customers of the fourteen major companies in both manufacturing and service industries serving both business-to-business markets and relationship-oriented consumer markets such as banking. It was found that:

■ Only 15 per cent of the customers switched their business to a competitor because they found a better product.
■ Only 15 per cent switched because they found a cheaper product.
■ 20 per cent switched because they had experienced too little contact and individual attention.
■ 49 per cent said they had switched because the attention they received was of poor quality.

Delivering service excellence

The customers were sending the following message from their behaviour, 'It is not just what you produce that matters, but how you deliver it also matters very much to us.' Many organizations started taking initiatives to listen to the voice of the customers. At a conference in October 1994, a speaker from Canon Europe NV highlighted various customer satisfaction surveys used in the European services operations. These included end-user customer satisfaction surveys and distribution satisfaction surveys. At the same conference a spokesman from Asea Brown Boveri AG (ABB) explained how his organization focuses attention on customers.

ABB's core businesses are power generation, power transmission and distribution, industrial automation and transportation. The strength of the group lies in the flexibility of the local units, compared with the benefits of belonging to a big organization.

The customer focus initiative started at ABB group level in 1990. Every business area had to create an overall approach which was to be introduced in all units world-wide. The three key elements of the approach were:

1. Continuous improvement of performance and process based on an interaction between time-based management, total quality management and supply management.
2. The results shall exceed the expectations of the customer and support ABB goals.
3. The approach shall be a substantial part of the strategy and completely integrated in all issues.

Regional and business areas work closely together. Figures 4.1 and 4.2 represent the customer focus model and the customer focus matrix of ABB.

There are a number of other examples of companies in the late 1980s and 1990s which have adopted 'focus on the customers' as a key aspect of their corporate strategy. SAS Airways is one such company.

Avis, the car hire firm, used to measure and monitor service by looking at the volume of complaints. They subsequently developed a tool to find out how many customers are being lost; the tool was the customer service balance sheet. It is based on periodic mail surveys of complaining and non-complaining customers. Avis's employees are told how well they are delivering service through the customer care income statement.

Management Ideas

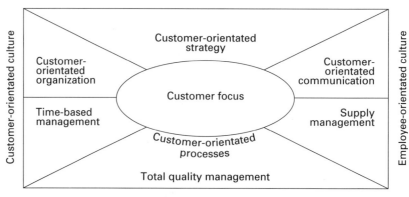

Figure 4.1 The ABB customer focus model

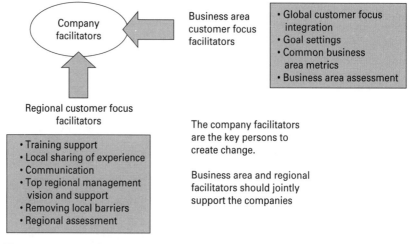

Figure 4.2 The ABB customer focus matrix

The customer care balance sheet tells the organization how much business they are losing both from customers who do not complain but who experience problems and from customers who do complain but are not satisfied with the way their complaints are handled. Data from the customer care balance sheet are then converted into annual lost sales or renewals.

Management gurus and the customer focus

Poor customer service can cost organizations millions of pounds. It is said that 90 per cent of unhappy customers do not complain but they do tell at least ten people about their bad experience or inadequate service. Based on this fact one can work out very simply the cost of losing one customer.

The focus on customer satisfaction has also been highlighted by numerous management writers. According to Rosabeth Moss Kanter, satisfied customers are the single best source of new business. According to Ohmae, in formulating business strategy it is important to pay painstaking attention to the needs of the customer.

In this section we will examine some of the views on customers expressed in the writing of two very influential management gurus of our time, Peter Drucker and Tom Peters.

Peter Drucker

Peter Drucker in his book *Innovation and Entrepreneurship*, published in 1985 under the heading of *Creating Customer Utility*, tells the story of Ronald Hill's invention.

Hill created utility. He asked: What do the customers need for a postal service to be truly a service to them? This is always the first question in the entrepreneurial strategy of changing utility, values and economic characteristics. In fact the reduction in the cost of mailing a letter, although 80 per cent or more, was secondary. The main effect was to make using the mails convenient for everybody and available to everybody. Letters no longer had to be controlled to 'epistles'. The tailor could now use the mail to send a bill. The resulting explosion in volume which doubled in the first four years and quadrupled again in the next ten, then brought the cost down to where mailing a letter cost practically nothing for long years.

He then goes on to give other examples of the companies who succeeded by listening to the customers:

Management Ideas

> Price in itself is not 'pricing' and it is not 'value'. It was this insight that gave King Gillette a virtual monopoly on the shaving market for almost forty years, it also enabled the tiny Haloid Company to become the multi-billion-dollar Xerox Company in ten years, and it gave General Electric world leadership in steam turbines. In every single case, these companies became exceedingly profitable. But they earned their profitability. They were paid for giving their customers satisfaction, for giving their customers what the customers wanted to buy, in other words, for giving their customers their money's worth.

In his book *The Practice of Management*, Peter Drucker wrote:

> If we want to know what a business is we must start with its purpose. . . There is only one valid definition of business purpose: to create a customer. What business thinks it produces is not of first importance – especially not to the future of the business or to its success. What the customer thinks he is buying, what he considers 'value' is decisive – it determines what a business is, what it produces, and whether it will prosper.

This passage was written forty years ago! We are still struggling to grasp the importance of listening to customers in order to survive and succeed in business. In another book, *Innovation and Entrepreneurship*, Drucker writes:

> 'But this is nothing but elementary marketing,' most readers will protest, and they are right. It is nothing but elementary marketing. To start out with the customer's utility, with what the customer buys, with what the realities of the customer are and what the customer's values are – this is what marketing is all about. But why, after forty years of preaching marketing, teaching marketing, professing marketing, so few suppliers are willing to follow, I cannot explain. The fact remains that so far, anyone who is willing to use marketing as the basis for strategy is likely to acquire leadership in an industry or a market fast and almost without risk.

Tom Peters

Tom Peters is co-author of *In Search of Excellence* and *A Passion for Excellence*, the first and second management books ever to rank number one on the *New York Times* national best-seller list. His book *Thriving on Chaos: Handbook for a Management Revolution* was published in 1987 and ranked on the *New York Times* list for over sixty weeks. His fourth book, *Liberation Management, Necessary Disorganisation for the Nanosecond Nineties*, was published in 1992 and in 1994. His latest book, *The Pursuit of Wow*, leapt straight into the business best-seller lists with phenomenal sales in the USA. It was released in Europe in 1995.

In all his books and seminars Peters makes competition and customers his core themes. In *Thriving on Chaos* he devotes a hundred pages to writing about customers. To Peters, service excellence has become the imperative of business success in the 1990s. The story of Nordstrom which appears in his book really drives the message home as far as delighting customers is concerned.

Nordstrom provides a superlative service to its customers. They provide very good service to their customers; the salespersons greet customers by name and with politeness. If you live in the West, says Peters, you can't talk about Nordstrom service because practically everyone has a bizarre Nordstrom story. Such stories are peppered throughout the writings of Tom Peters.

Putting focus on customers is not a new thing or a phenomena of the 1980s and 1990s. In studying marketing in the 1960s we learnt about consumer behaviour, consumer characteristics and meeting the needs of customers. Philip Kotler and Ted Levitt have been writing about the total product concept for a number of years.

As Drucker said, after almost half a century of preaching customer consideration, why is it that organizations are beginning to get excited now? The reason simply is intense competition. Business salvation in the 1990s lies in delivering product quality and service quality. It is not the question of 'either/or' but of delivering total quality. The organization consistently has to perform in the High-High box in Figure 4.3.

Management Ideas

Figure 4.3 Quality
matrix

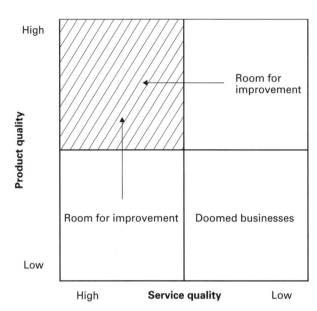

Surveys on customer service

Digital Equipment in association with John Humble, a management consultant, conducted a service survey in 1993. In this survey the two key questions asked were: 'How important is each factor in influencing your customers to buy your major product or service?' Quality was at the top of the list, followed by reliability, problem-solving, price (less emphasis in USA), speed of delivery, courtesy (more emphasis in Japan), after-sales service, design, guarantee and packaging.

When asked 'Where is there most room for improvement in your organization?', the response was in quality, speed of delivery, courtesy, problem-solving, reliability, after-sales service, price, design, packaging and guarantees.

The Forum Corporation undertook a research project in 1991 on the customer-focused quality company. The objective of the research project was 'to explore and illustrate the principles and actions required to lead and implement a customer-focused quality strategy'. Among the participants were organizations who have won the Malcolm Baldrige National Quality Awards and one participant was the recipient of the

Delivering service excellence

1989 Gold Award for Quality of the Canadian Awards for Business Excellence.

The findings of the Forum's research project were that:

- Organizations adopt a customer-focused quality strategy to stay ahead of competition and to survive in the changing business climate.
- Organizations that adopt a customer-focused quality strategy had to undergo a fundamental change in their beliefs and values. Everyone in the organization had to understand and live by new beliefs and values.
- Leaders 'live' their beliefs, communicate them via teams and act on their beliefs by investing in people.
- Leaders become 'the voice of the customers' in their organizations.
- Leaders realized customer-focused quality strategy is no 'quick fix'.

The survey conducted by Business International (the company owned by the Economist Group) in 1990 showed that the key drivers of corporate strategic directions were customer satisfaction, quality leadership and innovation. The key objectives of global organizational structure were customer responsiveness, profit orientation and quality.

In the 1980s and early 1990s, following the focus on customer service and customers' needs, many organizations initiated various projects to make heard the 'the voice of the customer'. Among such projects were:

- **Customer focus groups**: A panel of customers is interviewed about the company and their competitors; customers/prospects are invited to discuss particular topics, for example, on-time deliveries or product design.
- **Visits to customers**: Taking cross-functional groups from the organizations.
- **Customer councils**: Groups of customers who meet regularly to advise the company.
- **Questionnaires/postal surveys/telephone surveys**.
- **Customer research**: Organizations finding out who are their major customers, what proportion of business they represent, what are their growth prospects and the degree of relationship and contacts they have with the company.
- **Customer-care training**.

Self assessment

Those companies who have embarked upon self assessment quality initiatives and working along the lines of the European Quality Model have to demonstrate the organization's success in satisfying the needs and expectations of their customers.

The assessment is related to what the company is achieving in relation to the satisfaction of its external customers. Evidence is needed of the customers' perception of the company's products, services and customer relationships, and additional measures relating to the satisfaction of the company's customers. Twenty per cent of the total marks are assigned to meeting this result.

Evidence is required in terms of meeting product/service specifications, reliability, delivery, service performance, sales support, accessibility of key staff, responsiveness to customer needs, warranties/guarantees, value for money and fair treatment. Additional measures relate to repeat business, lost business, complaints, defect rates, delivery performance, awards received, publicity and so on.

External customers are defined as 'The immediate customers of the company and all other customers in the chain of distribution of its products and services through to the final customers'.

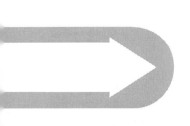

Case study: DHL International (UK) Ltd

Nick Butcher, managing director of DHL International (UK), presented a paper at the conference organized by the Economist Conferences at which he outlined how to change from providing 'lip service to true commitment'. In his view there are some very simple tactics that can be deployed to fulfil the objective of outstanding customer service. These are:

- Stay close to the customer.
- Decide close to the customer.
- Understand the customer.
- Manage the customer.
- Communicate with the customer.

He then went on to share some of DHL's experiences.

'Let me turn to 'staying close to the customer'. Until a few years ago DHL was a functionally driven organization where any given station or office would have someone responsible for managing the operations – the couriers, sorting and so on – and someone else responsible for managing sales. We decided to do away with this functional allocation of responsibilities and have attempted to create mini-businesses at the lowest possible level in order to take decision-making closer to the customers. This resulted in the creation of station managers, who in turn report to area directors. There are three area directors in the UK and they have very clear profit and loss responsibility, driven by customer retention and acquisition, and cost control. They are responsible for managing the pick-up from and delivery cycle to customers. As you can imagine, very tight objectives are set in this area.

In effect, we have decentralized a centralized structure. In the process we have eliminated several layers of management, moving from a structure where the managing director was seven levels away from the courier to one today where I am four levels away. We have organized our business so that a small business group has responsibility for customers and service in their areas.

All this is fine, but for any organization like this to work, 'decisions need to be made as close to the customer as possible'. This means that in our case a functionally managed organization had to devolve the power 'to decide' down the hierarchical chain to the lowest level possible. This was not easy and we still have some way to go in truly empowering our staff.

'Understanding customers': Listen and learn are the watchwords here. As with all market leaders, we study the marketplace very thoroughly, and invest heavily in research – both quantitative and qualitative – to gain a full understanding of the image and awareness of DHL in the marketplace but also of customers' satisfaction and needs.

Simple logic tells us that to serve customers well their needs should be thoroughly understood. Returning to the work of Treacy and Wiersema, their view is that it is vital to have an obsession with the process of solution development. Again fairly logical. The approach we have taken at DHL to gain a more in-depth understanding of our customers' wants is to use market research to build up a hierarchy of the needs of our customer-base.

Having established this hierarchy of needs, it's important to research how well a business is doing against them, and to change where necessary. Here is what our research tells us.

Management Ideas

'Managing customers' is another important ingredient, since during the lifespan of an account there is inevitably a shift in the demands a customer places on its suppliers. At DHL we call this our 'cradle to grave' philosophy.

'Cradle to grave' is an approach to communication planning which is responsive to the current requirements and potential of a customer as their relationship grows with a supplier.

As in any relationship – personal or business – there are various different phases. What 'cradle to grave' enables you to do is establish exactly where in the customer lifecycle you are currently sitting and to tailor your communications precisely to address that position.

Lastly, we need to 'communicate with customers'. This is obvious – but what and how and when are the more difficult questions to answer. The marketing slogans of the 1990s are 'database marketing' and 'relationship marketing'. Will these disappear? I don't think so, because I believe that whilst most companies will claim to employ these techniques, most only scratch the surface. Database marketing is really quite simple. It's using the information held about your customers, analysing it every which way to determine what they do with your product, why they do it, when they use it and so on. And who uses it. It does sound very simple but it isn't, yet harnessed to new technology, a very powerful market segmentation can be performed, like groups looked for and specific marketing campaigns devised.

Let me move on to employees. How many annual reports have you seen – or even written – that contain the following messages:

■ Our employees are our most valuable asset
■ Their commitment and loyalty are essential to the company's well-being, and
■ Thank you, to our employees, our result would not have been possible without you, etc.

But does this message have any impact on employees when their belief is that life is somewhat different?

■ You're expendable
■ We must cut costs if we are to maintain our leading position
■ Good bye.

That is the reality for most companies today, I am afraid.

Yet customer satisfaction starts with employee satisfaction.

As we look beyond the year 2000, business will be seeking at the very least to maintain profitability – and in most cases to grow it both in quantum and quality. I believe that a key element of any business strategy must be to achieve that state of mind amongst customers and employees – of loyalty.

Customer service policies will be one of the key tactics that will help in achieving this state. Think about it now because there are many already surfing the wave. Get up on your boards and go!

And finally service comes from people. All people make a difference – some positive – some negative. Informed and involved people make a positive difference.'

Abridged version. Full text appears in *Total Management Thinking* published by Butterworth–Heinemann in October 1996.

The presentation on DHL highlights the importance of technology, empowerment and trust on delivering customer service in an age of intensifying competition.

Why do some companies find it difficult to deliver service excellence?

- Some companies only like to pay 'lip service' to customer satisfaction.
- Some company policies are formulated for companies' convenience. (How often do we still hear 'I am sorry but it is not our company policy. . .'?).
- Many managers are remote from customers.
- Some companies believe that because they have a customer service department or a customer service manager they automatically become customer-driven companies.
- Many employees are not 'empowered' to satisfy customers.
- Many companies do not trust their staff to make decisions or resolve problems.
- Many organizations do not listen to their customers.
- Some organizations do not allocate enough resources to promote excellent customer service.
- Some employees who are still working for the organizations are psychologically retired or work under threat of

Management Ideas

being made redundant any day. (One such employee told me that his main concern is to check the company's noticeboard every Friday to see if his name appears under those sacked or made redundant – what a way to live!)

■ A number of organizations are excellent at appearing to care for their customers. Just because the organizations proclaim 'We are here to serve our customers' does not mean they do it.

Charles Handy in his book *Inside Organizations*, published by the BBC in 1990, relates the following story on the theme of how appearances can be deceptive.

Appearances can be deceptive

I was once asked to talk to a group of managers at the staff college of one of the large banks. It was our formal evening. Everyone was in suits, in rows, in upright chairs. They all wore their names and titles on their lapels. After I had spoken, the session was chaired, very formally, by the head of the college. I was placed for dinner at the top table between the head and his deputy. I never felt that I got close to the student managers or their problems. I mentioned this afterwards to the head and said that, in my view, such formality did not encourage frank discussion or any real learning, it was all just a kind of ritual.

Next time I went everything was different. This lot of managers were in casual dress. We sat in a large circle of armchairs and sofas. Drinks were available. Supper was a buffet affair. It was very informal and I enjoyed it immensely. I was staggered by the change. 'Is it always like this now?' I asked one of the young managers. 'Oh, no,' he said. 'Just today. Look.' and he showed me a paper pinned on the notice board headed 'Orders for the day'.

'In conformity with the wishes of our speaker tonight,' it read, 'dress will be informal and the session will be held in the Reading Room, not the Lecture Theatre, where drinks and supper will also be available. First names are to be used. These orders apply to this session only.'

'You see,' he said, 'it's all for you.'

Outward and visible signs do not always mean what they say.

Source: From *Inside Organizations* by Charles Handy with the permission of BBC World-wide Limited.

'Horror stories' of customer service

■ A customer wanted to buy a washing machine and visited one of the well-known distributors of electrical goods based in Croydon. She decided to spend nearly £500 to obtain a washing machine manufactured by a well-known brand name company. After she purchased the machine she was told by the sales assistant to purchase an extended warranty because these machines break down very often and it will be cost-effective to have an extended warranty.

Now I realize the assistant was keen to sell an extended warranty but to make such statements these days when all manufacturers are striving for product quality, is not and should not, be acceptable. How can manufacturers 'allow' distributors to discredit the products?

■ A shoe shop in London had a framed statement saying 'We care for our customers'. A foreign lady asked the sales assistant in this shop for size six shoes. The assistant went downstairs and fetched the shoes for the customer. After trying them on the lady said, 'I think I need one size bigger.' The assistant remarked, 'Lady I went down to get for you the size you wanted. I am not going to go up and down just because you cannot make up your mind.' What customer service!

■ A secretary in an insurance company which has been recently re-engineered told the customer she should speak to another department and explain her problem. When asked to transfer her call to the appropriate department she said 'I am sorry I do not have time to look for which department should handle your query and in any case it is not my job to keep on transferring calls to other departments. If I did so I will not be able to do my job.'

There are numerous other 'horror stories' of bad customer service provided by utilities companies, transport companies, well-known manufacturers and distributors. Reconciling such treatment to customers with alleged interest in customers by businesses is sometimes difficult.

Management Ideas

It pays to advertise?

in brief

"A tiger met a lion as they drank beside the pool.

'Tell me,' said the tiger, 'Why are you always roaring like a fool?'

'It's not so foolish,' said the lion with a twinkle in his eyes.

'They call me King of Beasts; it pays to advertise.'

A little rabbit overheard, and ran home like a streak.

He thought he'd try the lion's plan but his roar was just a squeak.

And a hungry fox that morning had his breakfast in the woods.

The moral: it does not pay to advertise unless you can deliver the goods."

Anonymous

Delighting customers

It does not matter how much emphasis is put on delivering good or excellent customer service, what matters at the end of the day is that people and especially front-line people in an organization have the feelings, will and commitment to serve the customers in a delightful way. One can set the procedures and produce award winning manuals but if the employees are treated badly or have bad feelings about the organizations they work for, or if they have the feeling 'I only work here', then all the efforts to deliver service excellence are going to be frustrated.

Commitment is a two-sided coin. On one side employees should give their full commitment to the organization they work for and subscribe to the organization's mission, and on the other side the organization has to give its commitment of employability, fair consideration and treatment to employees. This is the nature of the 'psychological contract' that exists between employees and employers nowadays. Without such a contract there will be neither people satisfaction nor customer satisfaction.

'Hearts and minds' of employees

Winning the hearts and minds of employees should be one of the strategic objectives of any organization. Many implementation strategies in practice miss this very vital fact. People-related issues are categorized as 'soft' issues and very often very little attention is paid to this aspect. If you research the main reasons for failures of total quality management or business process re-engineering it will boil down to people rather than structure or processes. Without leadership, commitment, competencies and trust, failures are guaranteed. Yet why is it that very little attention is paid to the people aspect in numerous books written on benchmarking, empowerment and business process re-engineering?

One of the key success factors on the people side should be the 'I'm OK. You're OK' factor. The 'I'm OK. You're OK' syndrome should relate to the feeling of employees towards their organizations and towards customers internally and externally.

Management Ideas

Eric Berne developed transactional analysis (TA) as a psychoanalytical approach to therapy. However, the ideas and techniques that it offers for looking at how we interact with others (colleagues, bosses, customers) are easily applied to everyday situations.

Interacting with others is a skill. Like any other skill it has to be understood, acquired and practised. Transactional analysis has some explanations on the nature of our behaviour and inter-personal transactions. According to transactional analysis theory three states exist within people. They are the child (C), the adult (A) and the parent (P).

The parent state consists of all the rules and the policies recorded from authority figures during childhood. (Think of something you do now which is just like something one of your parents used to do.) These messages are played back in different situations. Some of these messages assume a caring mode (I'm OK) and others a critical mode (I'm not OK). Quite often when we follow rules, procedures and the policies of the company and make sure our staff follow these as well, we are in 'parent ego state'.

The adult state is logical, reasonable and rational. It differentiates between the 'felt concept' of life in the childhood state and the 'taught concept' of life in the parent state. Behaviour in this state is characterized by problem-solving and rational decision-making. When employees are empowered and resolve problems on their own initiative they are in 'adult ego state'.

The child state is related to 'feeling'. People's behaviour in this state is driven by their feeling. ('I only work here' or 'My company does not care for me.')

All people behave from these three ego states at different times. The boundaries between these states are fragile and indistinct. There are three types of transactions, namely, complementary, crossed and ulterior. A complementary transaction is one in which the response comes from the ego state that was addressed.

A crossed transaction is one in which the response comes from a different ego state to that which was addressed. When a crossed transaction occurs, the interaction will not continue in the way intended by the first speaker.

An ulterior transaction includes an unspoken message in addition to the overt interaction. The recipient may respond to either, although the greatest psychological impact will be through the unspoken message.

Problems arise when transactions become crossed. In this situation individuals read things between the lines. When a manager says to the subordinate 'Can you do this properly', the subordinate immediately reads into this statement the implication 'You normally do not do it properly.'

Whenever people are transacting, be they at home or at work, 'strokes' are being exchanged. Strokes may be positive or negative and they are 'give-stokes' (giving) and 'get-strokes' (receiving).

In general people adopt the following life positions:

'I'm OK. You're OK.'
'I'm OK. You're not OK.'
'I'm not OK. You're OK.'
'I'm not OK. You're not OK.'

It is very useful to understand the importance of transaction analysis and to train employees in exchanging transactions and acquiring inter-personal skills. Open transactions facilitate effective communications but crossed transactions indicate the 'I'm not OK' feeling and it stops people listening to others (customers). To generate the 'I'm OK. You're OK' feeling, there has to be concern for self and concern for others. In relation to providing service excellence, the employee has to be in the 'I'm OK. You're OK' box in Figure 4.4.

Figure 4.4 Concern for self and customers

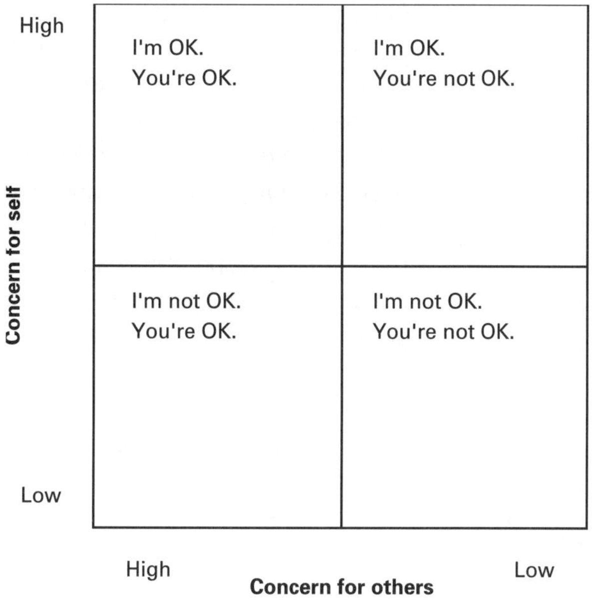

Management Ideas

Employees also view their situation from three perspectives. They are: What I like to do, What I have to do and What I am able to do. In Figure 4.4, the first area is where an employee feels joyful or 'I'm OK. You're OK.'

Trust is also the major driving force in injecting the 'I'm OK' feeling. It has become the most important factor in achieving effective empowerment. Trust has also become one of the key attributes of a successful leader in the 1990s.

Trust comes about when there is a series of positive encounters. Such positive encounters are characterized by allowing people to make mistakes, empowering your staff to make decisions, open communication and fair treatment. In the climate of downsizing and re-engineering, leaders and captains of industry have to work hard to win trust.

One way of earning trust is to make it very explicit in the strategy that the company cares for its customers and employees. Platitudes are not enough and often they backfire on organizations. Company strategy should explicitly reflect three dimensions. One dimension should reflect structure, products and processes to deliver corporate objectives, the second dimension should reflect customer service and the need to deliver service excellence and the third dimension should show concern for employees.

In a constantly changing environment some companies are now turning inward in search of 'soul' as a way to foster creativity and motivate leaders. An article in *Business Week* (June 1995) states that there is now a spirituality movement in the corporation and the object is to create a sense of meaning and purpose at work and connection between the company and the people.

What matters at the end of the day is not searching for 'soul' but the communion between the hearts and minds of the organization, employees and the customers. If enough attention is paid by the companies to make sure that their employees do not burn out and that they are valuable assets and create positive encounters and trust, then they will assume a position of 'I'm OK. You're OK' and service excellence will be delivered. Focus on personal development of employees is going to be the key differentiating factor for successful and excellent organizations in the late 1990s and the twenty-first century. As Sandra Vandermerwe, author of *From Tin Soldiers to Russian Dolls*, wrote: 'A focus on customers is an attitude rather than a task, a state of mind as opposed to a functional responsibility.'

Relationship marketing

Once employees' frame of mind is geared to customers, organizations can start building up long-term 'win-win' relationships with their key customers. According to Kotler, in relationship marketing, transactions move from being negotiated each time to being routinized. Profitability will be eventually enhanced by building and maximizing mutually beneficial relationships.

However, relationship marketing cannot be practised by all organizations. Some experts recommend relationship marketing with customers who have long time horizons and high switching costs.

in brief.

That's not my job

"This is a story about four people named Everybody, Somebody, Anybody and Nobody. There was an important job to be done to improve customer service and Everybody was sure that Somebody would do it. Anybody could have done it, but Nobody did it. Somebody got angry about that, because it was Everybody's job. Everybody thought Anybody could do it.

But Nobody realized that Everybody wouldn't do it. It ended up that Everybody blamed Somebody, when Nobody did what Anybody could have done."
Source unknown

Selected reading

Sarah Cook (1992) *Customer Care*. Kogan Page.
D.L. Gertz and J.P.A. Baptista (1995) *Grow to be Great*. The Free Press.
Thomas Harris (1973) *I'm OK – You're OK*. Pan Books.
Tom Peters (1992) *Liberation Management*. Macmillan, London.
Tom Peters (1995) *In Pursuit of Wow*. Vintage Books,
Sandra Vandermerwe (1993) *From Tin Soldiers to Russian Dolls*. Butterworth–Heinemann.
Richard C. Whiteley (1991) *The Customer Driven Company*. Century.
Various papers presented at 'Service Conference' 1995 organized by the Economist Conferences.

5

Business process re-engineering

in brief

"There is nothing more difficult to take in hand, more perilous to conduct, or more uncertain in its success than to take the lead in the introduction of a new order of things."
Unknown

Summary

■ Business process re-engineering is a fundamental rethinking and radical redesign of business processes to achieve 'quantum leap' improvements in business results.
■ The practice of re-engineering has become part of management vocabulary in the 1990s.
■ Hammer and Champy's view on business process re-engineering.
■ Dramatic improvements associated with business redesign. Even in Asia organizations have embraced the re-engineering initiatives.
■ Case study: Hall Mark.

Management Ideas

- Key characteristics and benefits of process re-engineering.
- Critical success factors.
- Why some business process re-engineering initiatives fail. Learning from other organizations' mistakes.
- How to re-engineer: a step-by-step guide.
- Approaches to change initiatives.
- Re-engineering and people.

Starting from scratch

Michael Hammer and Jim Champy's book *Re-engineering the Corporation* became the best-seller around the world as soon as it was published in 1995. People were buying this book to find out the nature of business process re-engineering (BPR) and what was so special about it. Some simply wanted to be assured that what they have been doing for a number of years in initiating changes in their organizations was indeed business process re-engineering.

To Hammer and Champy, business process re-engineering means reinventing or starting from scratch. It means throwing away all the rule books and old procedural manuals and discarding fundamental assumptions. According to Champy and Hammer, at the heart of BPR lies the notion of 'discontinuous thinking'.

Many organizations even today are built around Adam Smith's idea of division of labour. This involves the specialization and sub-division of tasks, the minimizing and standardizing of tasks and skills. The story of the division of labour in a pin factory as told by Adam Smith in his book *The Wealth of Nations* written in 1776 became not only popular but very influential. According to Adam Smith, division of labour brings about an increase of dexterity in every worker, it saves time and facilitates the invention of a great number of machines which enhance significantly each worker's productivity.

Initially Smith's idea was taken on board in the factories and subsequently it was extended to other businesses. Specialization led to compartmentalization of businesses into various divisions such as production, finance, marketing and sales. Many organizations, even today, are functionalized in this way.

The other movement which has left its mark in many organizations was the philosophy of scientific management led by Frederick W. Taylor. His book *The Principles of Scientific Management*, published in 1911, advocated the development of science of management with clearly stated rules and laws, scientific selection and training of workers and division of tasks and responsibilities between workers and management. Taylor recommended that there should be a detailed analysis of each job, using the techniques of method study and time study, in order to find the method of working that would bring about the largest average rate of production, the so-called 'one best way'.

He also advocated issuing detailed written instructions, training and incentive payments in order to ensure that jobs were performed in the approved manner.

Many of the assumptions implicit in the scientific management approach still have considerable influence on the design and organization of work. Such assumptions and outmoded rules have to be discarded completely for business process re-engineering to succeed. Business process re-engineering is the fundamental rethinking and radical redesign of business processes to achieve dramatic improvements in critical, contemporary measures of performance, such as cost, quality, service and speed. Hammer and Champy stress that the change must be **fundamental** and **radical**, the focus should be on **process** and the improvements must be **dramatic**.

Short glimpses of dramatic improvements due to re-engineering

- IBM Credit Corporation slashed seven-day turnaround to four hours without an increase in head count.
- Kodak re-engineered its product development process by introducing concurrent engineering. It introduced its new disposable camera in thirty-five rather than seventy weeks.
- Reuters slashed the time needed to respond to customers from weeks to days.
- The National and Provincial Building Society's chief executive officer David O'Brien created the 'process-driven organization'. He says 'The only thing you can do

in a volatile business environment is to create an organization that has the capacity to live in a permanent sate of change.'

■ Continental Canada Insurance embarked upon a re-engineering project which took fifteen months. Personal Automobile Insurance outperformed the industry average for profitability by 30 per cent. Twelve underwriters now do the work of sixty and 120 agents now service a more profitable base of service than 700 did previously.

■ A National Health Service trust in the UK has cut the cycle time from twelve weeks to less than a day. The trust wanted to reduce the time taken for an out-patient clinic to produce diagnostics to cut down administration costs and to increase the satisfaction of patients and staff involved.

■ AT&T Global Business reduced order processing ten-fold and achieved a 35 per cent reduction in headcount.

■ Bell Atlantic achieved a five-fold reduction in cycle time as far as customer services are concerned and the labour costs decreased from $88 million to $6 million.

■ Texas Instruments reduced process cycle time by well over 50 per cent.

■ Hall Mark cards reduced its new product development cycle from between two and three years to one year.

■ ABB, a Swedish-Swiss manufacturing giant, began re-engineering before the term was invented. It removed layers of management and halved the development time of its products.

■ *The Economist* of 23 October 1993 reported IBM's efforts to return to profit. It embarked upon re-engineering by examining all the operational 'processes' that take products from the drawing board to the customers. BPR became pivotal to IBM's success. New products are now designed around 'modules' which are interchangeable. This approach means fewer components and reaping economies of scale. Products are now updated more rapidly and cheaply.

■ At the Thai Farmers Bank customers are served within minutes instead of having to wait half an hour or more.

There are many other success stories related to Motorola, American Express, Proctor & Gamble and so on. The most quoted example of process re-engineering is the accounts receivable operation of the Ford Motor Company. The operation once employed 500 people shuffling purchase orders and invoices among themselves. Now 125 people do the same job faster. The clerk at the receiving dock, using a computer to reconcile orders instantly, accepts orders on his own authority and issues payment. No more paper shuffling! IT has become the real enabler for the introduction of radical change. IT can also play a key role in the mapping and analysis of processes.

The focus of BPR is on processes. A process is defined as 'a set of linked activities that take an input and transform it to create an output'. Processes in business are categorized into 'core' processes and 'support' processes. A core process creates value by the capabilities it gives the company from competitiveness. In practice it is alleged that there is a mismatch between business processes and the voice of the customer. There are many activities incorporated in the processes that have entered into business over time which do not add value to customers. In addition in many businesses today many barons are managing 'functional silos'.

Re-engineering in Asia

Re-engineering is not a Western business phenomenon. Many organizations in Asia have joined the management revolution. Re-engineering is being tried by banks, airlines, insurance companies, manufacturers and even some government departments.

The Thai Farmers Bank (TFB), according to *American Banker* magazine, spent $150 million to re-engineer its operations throughout 454 branches by the end of 1996. Apart from TFB, Shinhan Bank (one of South Korean's biggest banks), Dharmala Bank (an Indonesian Bank), Thai Airways International and Yamaha Motor Co. are all embarking on re-engineering initiatives.

Re-engineering is spreading in Asian organizations for three reasons:

- Improvement of customer service.
- To gain and retain competitive advantage.
- To make effective use of resources throughout the organizations.

What are the characteristics and benefits of business process re-engineering?

- Re-engineering integrates various tasks and activities into one.
- The steps in the process are performed in a natural order which is not necessarily linear.
- Work is performed where it makes most sense.
- Non-value adding activities are eliminated.
- There is no place for the 'command and control' type of management style.
- Processes are understood from the perspective of the customers.
- Full and open communication becomes important.
- It promotes 'rethinking' the nature and purpose of work.
- It restores respect for the individual.
- Work assumes multi-dimensional perspectives.
- Corporate and individual values change from being 'protective' to 'productive'.
- Smart work rather than hard work becomes the norm.
- Organizational structure becomes flat and 'functional silos' and 'functional stovepipes' disappear.
- Technology as an enabler becomes an important agent of business transformation and success.
- The organization's attention is focused on where to compete rather than how to compete.
- It promotes provocative culture – questioning everything an organization does and seeking innovative ways of doing work.
- It aligns core processes to business strategy.
- It promotes an organization's capability to adapt.

Discontinuous thinking

Business process re-engineering is not about automation or restructuring or downsizing. It is about a radical rethinking of ways of doing business in a changing environment. Of course 'managing change' has been a buzz word for a number of years now. In the past decade or so, numerous organizations have embarked upon the journey to change. But these change initiatives are being undertaken within the given functional structures and existing assumptions. The focus of attention is still on specialization. The changes undertaken have also been incremental – evolutionary changes rather than revolutionary changes.

Business process re-engineering creates revolutionary change. The change is 'radical' and the improvements are 'dramatic'. As far as business process re-engineering is concerned nothing is sacred. As one person put it, 'a company that has successfully been re-engineered itself is like a phoenix rising from the ashes'. Business process re-engineering asks fundamental questions about the processes a company is performing, the nature of the activities involved and whether significantly faster and more efficient and effective ways of achieving better results exist. Business process re-engineering is about 'quantum leap' change.

Figure 5.1 Change matrix

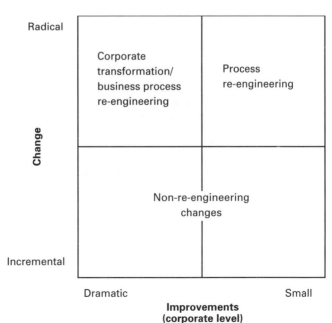

Management Ideas

In some organizations re-engineering is undertaken at one specific level, focusing on a group of processes rather than re-engineering processes across the organization. Some writers call such initiatives 'process re-engineering' in order to distinguish it from 'business process re-engineering'. There are some writers who refer to the re-engineering of the whole organization as 'corporate transformation' (see Figure 5.1).

Where a specific process or a group of processes is re-engineered and the change is radical and the improvements are dramatic at a specific level, but at organizational level the change is marginal, then the organization has been re-engineered. Where there has been a radical change throughout the organization and the improvements across the business are dramatic, then often the term used is 'corporate transformation'. This difference is important to keep in mind when readers are assessing or thinking about their situations and experiences.

Critical success factors of business process re-engineering

- There should be a desire to change the 'status quo'.
- There has to be trust, understanding, courage and above all patience.
- Top management must give their total involvement.
- Employees have to be empowered. Some writers say 'empowered' employees have to become 'renaissance' employees.
- Organizational structure must be flexible and responsive to customer needs.
- Culture has to be supportive 'allowing' risk-taking and not getting it right first time.
- Employees have to be trained in working in teams.
- Traditional assumptions have to be challenged.
- There should be considerable care taken in planning and implementation. Use technology as an enabler in bringing about a 'quantum leap'.

Why do some re-engineering initiatives fail?

According to the article which appeared in The *McKinsey Quarterly* 1994 (No. 2), some re-engineering initiatives have had paradoxical outcomes. There have been dramatic improvements in cycle time and process costs but still no impact on the bottom-line of the business as a whole. The article examined projects in more than 100 companies. The factors which have contributed to paradoxical outcomes have been found to be as follows:

- Re-design initiatives did not penetrate to the company's core and did not change roles and responsibilities, measurements and incentives, organizational structure, IT, shared values and skills.
- Process to be redesigned were not broadly based on cost or custom value.
- Senior executives did not invest enough time and energy.
- Focus on processes that were too narrowly defined.
- Inadequate identification of the activities to include in the process being redesigned that were critical for value creation in the overall business unit.
- Some companies wanted to minimize disruptions.
- In some cases there was a lack of good leadership to lead the organization through the period of change.
- There was resistance from various stakeholders.
- Not enough attention was paid to processes in those areas that fell short of customer expectations and competitive performance.

In addition to these factors some writers have noted the following contributions to re-engineering project failures:

- Lack of resources.
- Unreasonable expectations.
- Cynicism and scepticism.
- Stress and management burn-out.
- Lack of skills and adequate training.
- Poor teamwork.
- Bureaucracy.

Management Ideas

- Previous failures.
- Lack of strategy.

In an article in the *Harvard Business Review*, November–December 1993, entitled How To Make Re-engineering Really Work, the authors (Gene Hall, Jim Rosenthal and Judy Wade) highlight the following 'Five keys to a successful redesign' and 'Four ways to fail'.

Five keys to a successful redesign

The following five factors common to successful re-engineering efforts emerged from our study:

1. Set an aggressive re-engineering performance target. The target must span the entire business unit to ensure sufficient breadth. For example, aim for a $250 million pretax profit increase to result from a 15 per cent cost reduction and a 5 per cent revenue increase measured across the business unit as a whole.
2. Commit 20 to 50 per cent of the chief executive's time to the project. The time commitment may begin at 20 per cent and grow to 50 per cent during the implementation stage. For example, schedule weekly meetings that inform the top manager of the project's status.
3. Conduct a comprehensive review of customer needs, economic leverage points, and market trends. For example, customer interviews and visits, competitor benchmarking, analysis of best practices in other industries, and economic modelling of the business.
4. Assign an additional senior executive to be responsible for implementation. The manager should spend at least 50 per cent of his or her time on the project during the critical implementation stage.
5. Conduct a comprehensive pilot of the new design. The pilot should test the design's overall impact as well as the implementation process, while at the same time building enthusiasm for full implementation.

. . . and four ways to fail

There are any number of ways that a re-engineering project can fail. However, our study uncovered the following four particularly damaging practices:

1. **Assign average performance.** Companies tend to enlist average performers – most often from headquarters – for the project. Why? They reason that performance in the business unit will falter if they assign top performers to the redesign full time. For example, one company assigned a mediocre sales manager to head the project because he wouldn't be missed in the field. But because this manager lacked the credibility and skills to lead, the project ultimately failed.

2. **Measure only the plan.** Though most companies invest a lot of resources in estimating the effects of a redesign on cost, quality and time before implementation, they rarely follow through with a comprehensive measurement system that can track the new process's performance as it is actually being rolled out. Without this kind of measurement system, it is impossible to tell if and why implementation is succeeding or failing. A good tracking system should measure location-specific results and individual employee performance.

3. **Settle for the status quo.** Companies generally strive to develop redesign in ways that are radically new, but, more often than not, they never translate their aspirations into reality. Most companies have a difficult time thinking outside their own skill level, organizational structures, or system constraints. Moreover, companies that do come up with innovative approaches find them watered down by political infighting during the implementation stage. Incentives and information technology, in particular, can be politically sensitive areas.

4. **Overlook communication.** Companies always underestimate the level of communication that must occur during the implementation stage. They tend to use only one method of communication, like memos, speeches, or PR videos. More often than not, they neglect the more time-consuming but effective small group format in which employees can give feedback and air their concerns. It is essential to create a comprehensive communications program that uses a variety of methods of communication. It helps to assign a top-level manager to develop and implement an on-going communications program.

ACTION

How to re-engineer: a step-by-step approach

There are three stages involved in a re-engineering project. Each stage incorporates distinct activities.

Stage one

- Start with a clean sheet of paper and design all or part of the operations of a company.
- Look on the company as performing a small number of continuing processes rather than a collection of people performing specialized functions.
- Identify processes to be re-engineered.
- Define process boundaries.
- Prepare process maps.
- Distinguish between processes that have 'external' focus (customers, suppliers, distributors) and processes which have 'internal' focus (providing organizational capabilities).
- Distinguish between 'core' processes and 'support' processes.
- Decide on the importance and feasibility of the project.

Stage two – question time

- How are you going to do it?
- Who will be responsible?
- How should the project be managed?
- What are the baselines for measurement?
- What is the time-scale involved?
- How are you going to benchmark and with whom?
- What tools and techniques should be used?

Stage three

- Assemble a core team.
- Appoint a project manager.
- Identify board level champions.
- Start on the project.
- Keep open and full communication going all the time.

Business process re-engineering

The focus of re-engineering is processes. Core processes incorporate activities enhancing customer service, logistics, new product development, cash flow and communication. A core process allows customer needs to drive the way the company should do its business.

New product development core processes involve the following:

■ Generating project ideas
■ Proposition development
■ Test marketing
■ Launch preparation
■ Launch and establishment of product.

Activities involved are analysed according to the value-adding criterion and examined in terms of speed, flexibility, quality and deadlines.

Process mapping

Process mapping seeks to understand existing and possible future business processes in order to create enhanced customer satisfaction. In re-engineering the objective is to start with the boundaries of the process and look at how all elements need to be reconfigured. The most important thing to do before mapping processes is to agree on definitions of what constitutes a process, agree on activities involved and agree on a mapping approach.

The key questions to ask at this stage are:

■ What is it we are trying to do?
■ Why do we want to do it?
■ Who are we going to benchmark against?
■ How are we going to do it?
■ How will we know if we are on the right track?

Process mapping involves using charts to show process sequence. The simplest chart uses only operation and inspection symbols. The inspection generally is for quality. The set of symbols in common use are the ones developed by the American Society of Mechanical Engineers. A more comprehensive

Management Ideas

Figure 5.2 Activity symbols

Activity	Symbol
Operation	○
Inspection	□
Transport	➡
Storage	▽
Delay	D

version known as the flow process chart incorporates additional symbols. Figure 5.2 shows the symbols normally used.

There are many other techniques used to analyse processes, depending on the nature and complexity of the business in question.

The systems approach to change initiatives

Some writers recommend a systems approach to tackle redesigning business processes. The Open University Business School in their 'Planning and Managing Change' module put forward a technique of 'systems intervention strategy'. This technique has three overlapping phases:

- **Phase 1**: Diagnose the process by which you develop a way of tackling a particular set of change problems.
- **Phase 2**: Design the process which incorporates alternative methods of achieving change.
- **Phase 3**: Evaluate the options with 'change owners' and put an implementation plan in process.

The steps involved within the system intervention strategy are shown in Figure 5.3.

Figure 5.3 System intervention strategy. Source: The Open University Business School, Course B889

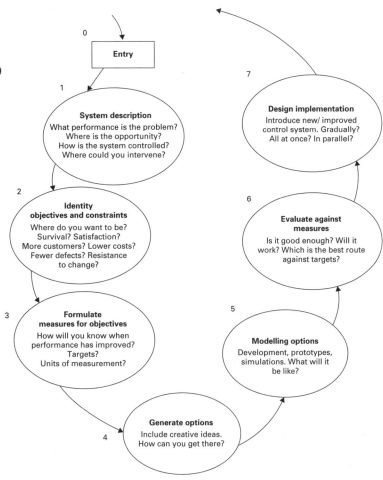

Table 5.1 shows the phases and steps involved and the action needed. **Iteration is needed in using this intervention strategy**.

Process re-engineering and the value chain

The other approach to change is to focus on the value chain. As Hammer and Champy have indicated, many organizations still operate in a traditional mode. The focus is still on the value chain, which has been popularized by Michael Porter.

Table 5.1 The three phases of strategy

1. Diagnosis
- 'Where are you now?'
- 'Where do you want to be?'
- 'How will you know when you get there?'

The steps of the strategy
0. Entry.
1. Description.
2. Identify objectives and constraints.
3. Formulate measures for your objectives.

What kind of actions are appropriate to each step?
- Start by recognizing that change is a complete process.
- Structure and understand the change in systems terms.
- Get other points of view on the change problem or opportunity.
- Set up some objectives for the systems which you are examining.
- Think of the objectives of the change itself.
- Decide on the ways of measuring whether an objective is achieved.

2. Design
- 'How can you get there?'
- 'What will it be like?'

The steps of the strategy
4. Generate a range of options.
5. Model options selectively.

What kind of actions are appropriate to each step?
- Develop any ideas for change as full options.
- Look at a wide range of possibilities.
- Your objectives may suggest new options.
- Describe the most promising options in some detail.
- Ask for each option: **What** is involved? **Who** is involved? **How** will it work?

3. Implementation
- 'Will you like it?'
- 'How can you carry it through?'

The steps of the strategy
6. Evaluate options against measures.
7. Design implementation strategies.
8. Carry through the planned changes.

What kind of actions are appropriate to each step?
- Test the performance of your option against an agreed set of criteria.
- Select your preferred options and plan a way of putting the changes in place.
- Bring together people and resources.
- Manage the process.
- Monitor progress.

Source: Course B889, 'Performance Measurement and Evaluation'. The Open University Business School.

The value chain categorizes a firm into its strategic relevant activities in order to understand cost behaviour and sources of differentiation. Every firm's value chain is composed of nine generic categories of activities which are linked together. The first five of these nine categories are inbound logistics, outbound logistics, marketing and sales and service. All of these constitute primary activities. The four categories of procurement, technology development, human resource management and the firm's infrastructure on the other hand constitute support activities. Organizations aim to achieve optimization of each element of the value chain. The focus is on the firm's activities and how value is added at each step of the value chain.

The concept of adding value is the key element of business process re-engineering. The focus is shifted from value chain to core processes and from product innovation to process innovation.

A firm is just a collection of activities such as order processing, sales force operations, etc., and the value chain is a way of analysing each activity in terms of the value it contributes to the business. At each level of a value chain one should analyse all the activities involved and obliterate activities which do not add value to a business in terms of enhancing profitability or customer satisfaction.

Whichever approach is adopted, in business process re-engineering the focus should be on business processes and their relationship with customers. Processes enhance business's operating capabilities which in turn enable them to implement new strategies and envision new strategic options. So re-engineering, apart from making the organization effective in terms of achieving strategic objectives, also opens up avenues for more strategic options.

What is wrong with re-engineering?

Changes normally produce causalities and re-engineering is no exception. According to the *Wall Street Journal*, it is estimated that if re-engineering continues at its present pace in US industry, there will be 2500 fewer managers by the end of the century. As one chief executive officer put it 'We are going on a journey. We will carry our wounded and shoot the stragglers.' What a way to motivate! How are the wounded cared for? Do stragglers not deserve better treatment?

Business process re-engineering has its critics. In his latest book, *The Pursuit of WOW*, Tom Peters writes, 'Today's re-engineering proponents match the religious zeal of yesterday's quality fanatics. And the idea is damned important. Decimating hierarchies via slash-and-burn strategies is one (big) thing. Re-engineering – linking up activities horizontally and reinventing key business processes – is quite another.' It's even revolutionary, as the re-engineering gurus claim.

Management Ideas

But it isn't the main game – at least the way re-engineering is being played by most companies. Like most quality programmes, re-engineering is mostly internally focused busywork, i.e. streamlining. While another necessary item in today's management arsenal, it is far from the whole story.

Prahalad and Hamel feel re-engineering has more to do with shaping up today's business than creating tomorrow's industries. Isaacs and Jones of the Boston Consulting Group believe that re-engineering itself needs a strategy.

The biggest criticism of re-engineering to date has been the point that far too much emphasis has been put on processes and very little consideration has been given to 'soft' issues of business, in particular in relation to people. In this vein a very interesting article was written by Gareth Rees, chief executive of Kinsley Lord Management Consultants, which appeared in the journal *Focus on Change Management*, February 1994. The article is reproduced below:

The people versus re-engineering

Lawyer for the plaintiff: 'Ladies and gentleman of the jury, you are here to consider a most serious case – that a juggernaut called re-engineering (an approach to redesigning the way tasks are carried out in a firm) has inflicted psychological and social harm on my clients, the employees and staff of Cosyfirm Ltd. Our case is not that re-engineering is intrinsically bad. Indeed, my clients had hoped that in addition to improving efficiency, it would also improve the quality of their working lives. Our case is that the company has been negligent in the way in which it has applied re-engineering, and as a result has failed to achieve some of the objectives and has increased the stress and reduced the quality of the lives of its employees. Re-engineering was introduced to the company eighteen months ago and is now largely complete. As our witnesses will acknowledge, it has produced real benefits for Cosyfirm and its customers. But they will also testify to the unnecessary pain and stress it has caused them as people, the damage to their self-esteem and the opportunities lost to the firm, because their skills and knowledge have not been tapped to the full. Let me call my first witness.'

Business process re-engineering

Witness 1: Head of engineering

'I am still called the head of engineering at Cosyfirm, though my job is a pale shadow of what it was. For me, re-engineering has been a disaster.

'As a member of the management team I went along with the decision to re-engineer. We were too set in our ways and our poor competitive performance meant that we had to do something. The consultants were plausible, though some of their jargon was difficult to understand, and the CEO seemed convinced. If we had known how much pain it was going to cause, I am sure we would have thought twice.

'I used to run a tight engineering department. All of my people knew what was expected of them; we had standards and ways of doing things. True, we had our battles with production and R&D but we knew how to sort them out. We were making progress. Rather than build carefully on this, we had a revolution, and a painful one at that.

'The new production and product department process teams are not a bad idea. But with this new organization my craftsmen are spread out among processes and it's almost impossible to maintain standards. Technical training is falling by the wayside because I can't insist they attend. Functional expertise that took us years to develop will probably be lost. There's a timebomb of falling competence here. If it continues, quality will drop and so will sales.

'We are obsessed with IT. Company-wide access to a single database sounded great, but we're bending lots of things to make IT work. It costs a fortune and is not as flexible as we hoped. Given our obsession with IT, it's no wonder we didn't think enough about the human side of re-engineering.

'I cringe when I think back. We were in panic when we realized just how many people were being shaken out – we had no severance scheme or re-training ready. They didn't know what hit them. I felt useless and incompetent for the first time in my life, morale has not recovered.'

Witness 2: Sales representative

'I have been responsible for our sales to the pharmaceutical industry for the past four years. The re-engineering exercise has brought some real benefits to my customers, mostly in reduced delivery times. I guess our costs are coming down a little, so perhaps the sales force won't have to negotiate so many unpopular price increases.

Management Ideas

'There are some drawbacks, though. Everything is OK when we are having a good quality production run, but if a customer wants something special, or a product goes off spec., it seems to take longer to get things changed or fixed. We'll have to pull our socks up or we will let our competitors in.

'Part of the problem is that my old network of contacts has gone – they've either left or are doing different jobs. It's hard to get to the source of the problem because everything seems so fluid with all these teams. I can't even get Alice, the sales office administrator, to chase things up, she's too busy working with sales/production scheduling.

'That's another thing. A common database across the company is great in theory; the trouble is we miss the tweaking that Bert used to do. He knew what was doable and what wasn't, and kept the nonsense out. Unfortunately, Bert's intuition was re-engineered away.

'As I talk through this I'm beginning to realize why I'm feeling stressed. The firm feels more automated. There is less flexibility and less care. The new system has a hierarchy of its own – a system hierarchy, rather than the old command hierarchy. I can't seem to influence things as much now. I feel more lonely, just when I thought teamwork would make the place more human and flexible.'

Witness 3: Team leader

'I was a foreman in sub-assembly but now I'm production team leader. My job hasn't changed much in some ways – I still have to make sure we hit our production quota – but in others it's changed a lot. We make more of the finished product now and I don't know this team so well. I'm not used to maintenance people in the team, and being responsible for our own QA is frightening.

'We found it difficult to understand what they wanted us to do to start with but we're getting the hang of it. They changed our production methods to reduce waiting and tool changing times, formed us into new teams, set us targets and told us to work together to improve output and quality. We're not getting on badly now, but management made a pig's ear of introducing the new system. First, no one told us what was happening, we got no warning. Then they turned up with a bunch of consultants who generally ignored us, kept appearing and disappearing, and held endless mysterious meetings with management. They brought in these new production methods, which didn't work until we sorted them ourselves. Why didn't they ask us in the first place?

'It was bedlam for months. We lost a lot of output, not only because the new production process didn't work but because the blokes were too tee-ed off to bother. I don't think they'd heard of motivation, the lot of them. If the blokes were really switched on we'd move into another gear, find ways of sorting out problems quicker and add at least 15 per cent to output.

'It's the production managers, what's left of them, that I feel most sorry for. They had little to say on the changes, and because we're supposed to solve our own problems, they're lost. How can you turn a sergeant major into a football coach overnight? Somebody had better show them how before all their hair falls out.'

Witness 4: Fitter

'This lot in my new process team are space-cadets. I don't know what they are talking about half the time. Mary from marketing, Alistair from new product development, Susan from sales; it's kids, holidays and playgroups – what happened to sex and football and sex? No one takes the mickey and there's no-one to take the mickey out of.

'This high performance team, as they call it, ain't perform-ing much and ain't much fun. True, we did sort out the Johnson's new product prototype problem quickly, but that was more by luck. Having Ralph, the engineer, and Alistair on the same team saved the usual to-ing and fro-ing; but we hardly knew each other, had different ways of tackling a problem and seem to speak different languages. It was a bit of a miracle we hit on an answer.

'When they set up the team we got no help from the managers, who seemed as confused as we were. We were just told that we were a new team whose job it is to streamline and speed up new product introduction, and left to get on with it. No training, no game plan, no organization. If I ran the Angling Club like that we wouldn't catch a sprat, and I'd have a mutiny on my hands.

'We can't fiddle the overtime like we used to, but I still spend half the shift waiting for parts or waiting for Fred to wire up a plug. I could have finished it and gone home hours ago. I miss my mates, but not Harry, the foreman. At least I don't have him checking up on my every nut and bolt.'

Management Ideas

Witness 5: Process development owner

'Getting involved in the re-engineering exercise at the outset, especially as 'process owner', was great for me. I'm doing an MBA part-time, specializing in corporate change, so it's given me first-hand experience. I've come to a number of conclusions about BPR as we applied it.

'One of the most obvious differences from the theory of change is that we missed the 'unfreezing' phase – helping people to understand the reason for change and the benefits that would flow from it, and giving them time to get used to the idea and prepare for it. Once the management made a decision to go ahead we formed process teams, looking across the business to the customers rather than reporting vertically to the boss, and got started. People couldn't understand why 'if it ain't broke' we were fixing it. We failed to make the case for change and gather enough support. It was an uphill task as a result.

'From the outset, I struggled to get my managerial colleagues to commit enough resources to the job. They seemed to think it could be added onto the week's work and that substitutes would do. It created a lot of friction and unhappiness. As a result we didn't involve properly the people who really do the nitty-gritty – so we didn't benefit from their ideas; it was a constant struggle between the process teams and the functional line people – and still is.

'We've got it going now, but it's a curate's egg. The main manufacturing process works best. It seems to lend itself to this sort of approach – a straightforward flow of material operations through the factory, easy to measure progress and variances. I don't think though, that we have really improved quality of life. Somehow, we've reinvented the worst aspects of Taylorism in designing repetitive, non-thinking jobs. The textbooks say that we should re-design operations to take account of social and technical factors. I think the technical bias caused us to miss important people aspects.

'I have tried to rectify that in the product development process, but we've had trouble redesigning the way we work. I called the consultants back, they followed us around the iterative loops that product development inevitably takes, and have now announced that it is very difficult. Apparently, current re-engineering techniques don't work well on 'non-linear' processes. Great ammunition for my MBA dissertation, but useless in sorting me out.'

Business process re-engineering

Summing up

'Ladies and gentlemen of the jury, the evidence is clear. Through lack of thoughtfulness, indeed negligence given that thought is management's prime duty, Cosyfirm's employees have been seriously hurt. They have suffered needless pain, stress and even hardship. The firm has failed to reap the maximum benefit from what is a very valuable concept, largely as a result of mishandling people issues. The witnesses have given you first-hand accounts of the damage inflicted. The failures were:

- in not fully understanding the implications of the re-engineering exercise; could they not have explored the implications thoroughly before committing themselves?
- in not communicating the case for change and enlisting the support of people; could they not have demonstrated the likely impact of future competitive pressure? Didn't they think that staff would see it?
- in being seduced by the possibilities offered by IT and being blind to the importance and needs of people; why did they not pilot test the solution?
- in not preparing adequately for severance and retraining; the damage to morale is directly hurting the firm itself through reduced levels of initiative;
- in not working out how to maintain functional competence when re-organizing along process lines; can you hear the time-bomb ticking?
- in not being sensitive and responsive to mistakes; by not building in simple problem solving routines which ensure learning from past experience;
- in designing a new order which does not make the best use of the knowledge and skills of staff; they dumped problems on staff rather than developing them as empowered teams, and expected high performance.

'Management has driven re-engineering like a juggernaut through the firm, unnecessarily hurting its people and not achieving the full benefits. Ladies and gentlemen, I ask you to find the defendants guilty and award substantial damages to my client.'

By Gareth Rees, CEO, Kinsley Lord. First published by Armstrong Publications Ltd in *Focus on Change Management*. © 1994.

...in brief   **Management Ideas**

The article very clearly demonstrates the point that in any change initiative, be it total quality management, re-engineering business processes or working in teams the most important way to gain understanding, involvement and commitment is to pay attention to employees in terms of training them, trusting them and being honest in open communication. **Success ultimately depends on PEOPLE**.

Selected reading

Gerard Burke and Joe Peppard (eds) (1995) *Examining Business Process Re-engineering*. Kogan Page.

The Economist Intelligence Unit/Anderson Consulting Report (1995) Business Re-engineering in Asia.

Michael Hammer and James Champy. (1995) *Re-engineering the Corporation*. Nicholas Brealey.

Henry J. Johansson, Mchugh, Pendlebury, Wheeler III (1993) *Business Process Reengineering*. John Wiley.

Richard K. Lochridge (1994) *After Re-engineering: Organizing for Growth*. Chilmark Press.

Management Review (1995) Re-engineering: Tales from the Front. January.

Management Review (1995) Why Re-engineering Fails. July.

Performance measurement

in brief. "To become what we are capable of becoming is the only end in life." **Robert Louis Stevenson**

Summary

■ Performance measures are necessary for organizations because they show if organizations are achieving their targets set at strategic and operational levels.
■ Business results have to be measured and monitored regularly.
■ Performance can be focused on products, processes and people (employees and customers).
■ Performance measures have quantitative and qualitative dimensions.
■ Financial performance measures/sources of financial information: balance sheet, profit and loss account, applications and sources of funds.
■ Financial ratios in a nutshell.
■ Organizational performance: economy, efficiency and effectiveness.
■ Measuring customer service.
■ The balanced score card approach.
■ Staff appraisal and associated problems.
■ Designing performance appraisal.
■ Three-hundred-and-sixty-degree feedback: key success factors.
■ How do you rate as an employee? Your SWOT analysis.

Measuring performance

All organizations formulate strategies to determine the direction of their businesses. At a strategic level the fundamental questions asked are What business do we want to be in? How are we going to achieve our mission? What kind of competencies and structure do we need to meet our objectives? and finally What is the time scale of achievement? Strategic decisions determine the direction of business and tactical decisions decide the nature and the type of operations

Having set up the direction and the operations, the next stage is to formulate performance measures to assess the progress. In some situations being on the right track is not good enough. Businesses have to move faster in order to remain competitive. It is very important to measure progress against the objectives set. There is a need for regular monitoring and review. If there are any adjustments to be made we have to make quick decisions to get back on track. Control, therefore, is an integral part of business management (see Figure 6.1).

Figure 6.1 Control loop

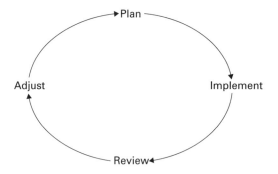

Performance management is about setting standards of performance and tracking performance to monitor business results consistent with business objectives. Performance can be focused on processes, products and people (customers, employees); see Figure 6.2. Unfortunately in practice many organizations focus on financial performance and pay very little attention to processes and people. Financial performance is one of the dimensions of performance measurement.

118

Figure 6.2 Dimensions of performance

Measuring financial performance

in brief "What gets measured gets done."
"When conflicts arise, financial considerations win out."

Organizations at the end of the day have to make profits and remain solvent. This is the expected outcome by all the stakeholders of the organization.

There are three sources of financial information as far as organizations in the private sector are concerned. These sources are the balance sheet, profit and loss account and sources and application of funds.

Balance sheet

The balance sheet is a financial situation showing what a company owes (its liabilities) and what the company owns

Management Ideas

(its assets) at a given point of time. It is a financial snapshot of a company. It gives information on capital (share and loan capital), current liabilities (creditors, taxation, dividends, overdraft), fixed assets (plant, buildings, machinery, equipment) and current assets (stock, debtors and cash).

Current assets minus current liabilities gives information on the working capital. The management of working capital is the lifeblood of business. Figure 6.3 shows the working capital cycle.

Figure 6.3 Working capital cycle

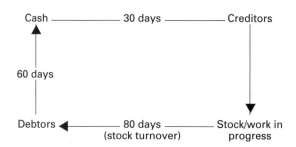

In Figure 6.3, cash is locked in for 110 days (80 days + 60 days − 30 days). The size of the net figure for working capital has a direct effect on the liquidity of a company. The return on capital employed is also affected by the level of working capital; the higher the investment in working capital, the lower will be the return on capital employed.

From the balance sheet one can measure stock days, debtor days, creditor days, asset turn, short and long term liquidity ratios, gearing ratio and the return on capital employed.

- **Stock days** (Debtors/Cost of sales × 365): This gives an indication of the number of days' sales for which payment is outstanding.
- **Debtor days** (Debtors/Sales × 365): This gives an indication of the number of days' purchases for which payment is still due. The credit taken from suppliers is a source of short term finance.
- **Asset turn** (Sales/Capital employed): This ratio tells us how many £ of sales are generated each year for every £ of capital employed.
- **Acid ratio** (Debtors + Cash/Current liabilities): This shows the company's ability to finance immediate liabilities.
- **Current ratio** (Current assets/Current liabilities): This shows what resources are available to meet the liabilities.

■ **Gearing ratio** (Total debt/Shareholders' funds × 100): This gives an indication of the ability of the company to finance its operations in the long term.

■ **Return on capital employed (ROCE)** (Operating profit (or profit before interest and tax)/Capital employed (fixed and current assets): This tells us how management has used the total funds available to the business; it measures its earning power. Value is only added to the business if it earns a higher ROCE than the rate of interest it pays or would pay on borrowings. If ROCE is less than the cost of borrowing then the money would be better invested elsewhere.

There are also other measures such as return on equity (Profit after tax/Ordinary shareholders' funds) and return on net assets (Profit before interest and tax/Net assets). These are both return on investment (ROI) measures.

Profit and loss account

The second source of financial information is the profit and loss account. It shows how the company has traded in the year it is reporting. From the information given one can measure sales growth, gross margin (Gross profit/Sales × 100), operating margin, sales per employee and operating profit per employee.

Sources and application of funds

The final source of information is sources and application of funds. This tells us where the money in the business has come from (sources) and how it has been spent (application).

Financial performance measures highlighted so far fall under the categories of profitability, solvency and financial structure. These are shown in Table 6.1.

Finally, as far as financial measures are concerned, there are measures from the stock market perspective such as earnings per share (Profit after tax/Number of ordinary shares issued), and price/earning ratio (Market price per share/earning per share).

Management Ideas

Table 6.1 Financial performance measures

Profitability	Solvency	Financial structure.
ROCE	Acid ratio	Gearing ratio
Return on assets	Current ratio	
Return on investment		
Profit margin		
Profit per employee		

Performance is not simply measured by financial targets though many businesses obsessively measure short term financial performance in their budgeting and forecasting cycles. Many executives are constantly involved in such corporate financial 'rituals'.

There are other forms of performance measures depending on what is being assessed. For example, the sales department might measure volume of sales by value, product, customer (key accounts), invoice, country, distributor or region.

Traditionally performance measures grew from financial reporting systems. Financial performance measures still dominate and preoccupy many organizations. According to the Economist Intelligence Unit's research conducted in association with KPMG (1994), most companies still track profits, earnings per share and growth in sales as key performance indicators of their businesses. The same report concludes that more than 70 per cent of the respondents feel dissatisfied with the company's performance measure system.

Obsession with financial performance – counting rather than measuring

Case study – Company A

Company A is a book publishing company based in London and New York. Its annual turnover is £50m. The company is divided into four product divisions namely, Science, Social Science, Business and Arts. It also has a small training division providing public seminars on taxation issues.

Performance measurement

In December each year all divisions are asked to think about their business goals for the following year and start putting together total revenue figures and propose gross margins. This process continues throughout December until mid-January. The managing director then issues revenue and total costs figures for all divisions to achieve during the year. These figures are extrapolated from past performance without analysing the causes behind the performance. This is 'performance management by extrapolation'.

From mid-January until the end of February, divisional managers have to come up with detailed information on how the revenues and the costs figures prescribed by the managing director are going to be achieved and, in consultation with the IT department, volumes of spreadsheets are produced.

In March each division has budget reviews and significant pressures are put on divisional managers to propose prescribed revenues and costs. When this is done all the divisional budgets are submitted to the management committee. The budget submissions are then fine-tuned and finally submitted to the management board in April.

In July each divisional manager is asked to forecast their financial performance for the period May-June-July – the first quarter of the financial year – and provide commentaries on forecasted performance. All the forecasts are then discussed by the management committee. At this stage, again, considerable pressures are put on the divisional managers who are forecasted to under-perform financially. The first quarter financial forecasting finishes in July.

In October, January and April, second, third and fourth quarter forecasting begins. Meanwhile from January the following year's budget process begins and all the managers go through the same 'corporate rituals'.

In between these periods, so that the people aspect of performance is not forgotten, all business managers are asked to conduct appraisals for their staff. Managers view such practice as an intrusion to their work and, therefore, they try 'to get over' staff appraisals as soon as possible.

No performance appraisal is done on any qualitative dimension, nor is serious attention paid to the reasons behind the financial performance. Financial results tell you the 'what' but not the 'why' of performance.

There are other dimensions of performance that this company should pay attention to. Unfortunately, because Company A is doing very well financially, the management think they have got it right. It is unfortunate because the people development aspect is ignored and there is lack of enthusiasm and motivation for managers to over-perform under this culture.

In the long run Company A will suffer financially and it will be too late to save it!

Dimensions of organizational performance

Organizations can measure performance from the point of view of **economy, efficiency** and **effectiveness**. Economy focuses attention on the cost of the inputs used. Efficiency focuses on the relationship between inputs and outputs (productivity), whereas effectiveness relates to achieving results consistent with corporate objectives.

- Economy means 'doing it cheap'.
- Efficiency means 'doing it right'.
- Effectiveness means 'doing the right thing right'.

Organizations have to formulate measures of effectiveness which involve measuring and monitoring corporate objectives and how these objectives are being implemented and monitored.

Performance measures in relation to quality

Chapter 2 dealt with criteria as applied to the Malcolm Baldrige National Quality Award. To win this award requires measuring performance in seven areas, namely, leadership, information and analysis, strategic quality planning, human resource utilization, quality assurance of products and services, quality results and customer satisfaction. Different points are allocated for each category and measures are performed to determine the level of achievement.

In relation to the European Quality Award, nine areas are designated for assessment. They are leadership, people management, policy and strategy, resources, processes, people satisfaction, customer satisfaction, impact on society and business results. Again points are allocated against each 'enabler' and 'result' and assessment is made as to the level and degree of achievement.

Measuring customer service

In delivering service excellence, organizations measure repeat business, lost business, number of complaints, defect rates, delivery time, and so on. Measures of customer needs and satisfaction are facilitated by visiting customers and finding out their needs, forming customer focus groups, issuing questionnaires, conducting customer research, and so on. In Chapter 4 we have seen how DHL measures customer service in order to improve the performance of its businesses.

Balanced scorecard approach

The balanced scorecard approach was proposed by Robert Kaplan, professor of accounting at Harvard Business School, and David Norton, president of Renaissance Strategy Group, a consulting firm. The advantage of this approach is its comprehensiveness in measuring various dimensions of business and the way it translates corporate strategic objective into a 'coherent set of performance measures'.

Measurement focuses on four dimensions of business, namely financial indicators, customer performance, internal processes and innovation and learning. By selecting a limited number of critical indicators under each perspective, the scorecard helps focus the strategic vision.

The type of scorecard approach used will depend on the nature of organization and the business it is in. Manufacturing businesses would adopt a different approach, for example from service industries. According to Michael Morrow, a consultant at KPMG, the balanced business scorecard is now widely used as a framework for the whole business. The first significant application in Europe was by Aer Lingus and the largest to date is NatWest. The balance business scorecard aims to provide performance measures at strategic level, business unit level, process level and individual level.

From a financial perspective, a business can measure its growth, liquidity, shareholder value, cash flow, return on capital employed and other significant indicators. From an internal business perspective, the measures could focus on cycle time, unit cost, defect rate, safety rate and other operational variables. From an organizational learning perspective, one would assess technological capability, time to market, new product introduction, rate of improvement, employee attitude, etc. And from a customer perspective, the measures would relate to assessing market share, customer satisfaction, supplier relationship/partnership, key accounts and so on (see Figure 6.4).

Robert Kaplan and David P. Norton in their article Putting the Balanced Scorecard to Work, published in the *Harvard Business Review*, September–December 1993, give the following advice on building a balanced scorecard.

Building a balanced scorecard

Each organization is unique and so follows its own path for building a scorecard. At Apple and AMD, for instance, a senior finance or business development executive, intimately familiar with the strategic thinking of the top management group, constructed the initial scorecard without extensive deliberations. At Rockwater, however, senior management had yet to define sharply the organization's strategy, much less the key performance levers that drive and measure the strategy's success.

Companies like Rockwater can follow a systematic development plan to create the balanced scorecard and encourage commitment to the scorecard among senior and mid-level managers. What follows is a typical project profile:

1.   Preparation

The organization must first define the business unit for which a top-level scorecard is appropriate. In general, a scorecard is appropriate for a business unit that has its own customers, distribution channels, production facilities and financial performance measures.

Performance measurement

2. Incentive: first round

Each senior manager in the business unit – typically between six and twelve executives – receives background material on the balanced scorecard as well as internal documents that describe the company's vision, mission and strategy.

The balanced scorecard facilitator – either an outside consultant or the company executive who organizes the effort – conducts interviews of approximately ninety minutes each with the senior managers to obtain their input on the company's strategic objectives and tentative proposals for balanced scorecard measures. The facilitator may also interview some principal shareholders to learn about their expectations for the business unit's financial performance, as well as some key customers to learn about their performance expectations for top-ranked suppliers.

3. Executive workshop: first round

The top management team is brought together with the facilitator to develop the scorecard. During the workshop the group debates the proposed mission and strategy statements until a consensus is reached. The group then moves from the mission and strategy statement to answer the question, 'If I succeed with my vision and strategy, how will my performance differ for shareholders; for customers; for internal business processes; for my ability to innovate, grow and improve?'

Videotapes of interviews with shareholder and customer representatives can be shown to provide an internal perspective to the deliberations. After defining the key success factors, the group formulates a preliminary balanced scorecard containing operational measures for the strategic objectives. Frequently, the group proposes far more than four or five measures for each perspective. At this time, narrowing the choices is not critical, though straw votes can be taken to see whether or not some of the proposed measures are viewed as low priority by the group.

4. Interviews: second round

The facilitator reviews, consolidates and documents the output from the executive workshop and interviews each senior executive about the tentative balanced scorecard. The facilitator also seeks opinions about issues involved in implementing the scorecard.

Management Ideas

5. Executive workshop: second round

A second workshop involving the senior management team, their direct subordinates, and a larger number of middle managers, debates the organization's vision, strategy statements, and the tentative scorecard. The participants, working in groups, comment on the proposed measures, link the various change programs under way to the measures, and start to develop an implementation plan. At the end of the workshop, participants are asked to formulate stretch objectives for each of the proposed measures, including targeted rates of improvement.

6. Executive workshop: third round

The senior executive team meets to come to a final consensus on the vision, objectives and measurement developed in the first two workshops; to develop stretch targets for each measure on the scorecard; and to identify preliminary action programs to achieve the targets. The team must agree on the implementation program, including communicating the scorecard to employees, integrating the scorecard into a management philosophy, and developing an information system to support the scorecard.

7. Implementation

A newly formed team develops an implementation plan for the scorecard, including linking the measures to databases and information systems, communicating the balanced scorecard throughout the organization, and encouraging and facilitating the development of second-level metrics for decentralized units. As a result of this process, for instance, an entirely new executive information system that links top-level business unit metrics down through shopfloor and site-specific operational measures could be developed.

8. Practical reviews

Each quarter or month, a blue book of information on the balanced scorecard measures is prepared for both top management review and discussions with managers of decentralized divisions and departments. The balanced scorecard metrics are revisited annually as part of strategic planning, goal setting and resource allocation processes.

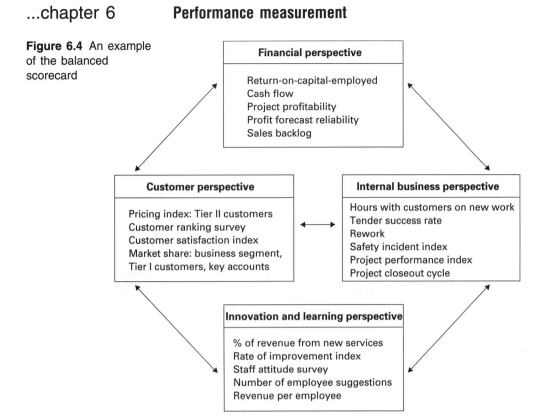

Figure 6.4 An example of the balanced scorecard

Financial perspective

Return-on-capital-employed
Cash flow
Project profitability
Profit forecast reliability
Sales backlog

Customer perspective

Pricing index: Tier II customers
Customer ranking survey
Customer satisfaction index
Market share: business segment,
Tier I customers, key accounts

Internal business perspective

Hours with customers on new work
Tender success rate
Rework
Safety incident index
Project performance index
Project closeout cycle

Innovation and learning perspective

% of revenue from new services
Rate of improvement index
Staff attitude survey
Number of employee suggestions
Revenue per employee

Measuring staff performance

Staff appraisals are conducted in many organizations. The objective of such appraisals should be to motivate behaviour leading to continuous improvement. Speaking to many business executives, they feel that in most cases staff appraisals are ineffective because they are not done properly. Some staff find them very intimidating 'corporate rituals' they have to go through annually.

There are four categories of problems associated with performance appraisals. These are the measurement problem, the judgement problem, the organizational problem and the design problem.

The measurement problem

Some organizations find it very difficult to decide what to appraise due to the lack of understanding of the roles and responsibilities involved or due to the ambiguity of roles involved. In some cases measures formulated are inadequate because not enough thought has gone into designing them.

In some cases there is confusion between a behaviour-based performance indicator and competency-based performance.

The judgement problem

Many managers do not like to act as a judge. There are numerous examples in practice to show disagreement on ratings, different interpretations put on different indicators by appraisee and appraiser. Biases also creep in when judgements are made on the behaviour-based indicators and some find it very uncomfortable to assess their subordinates especially when they have to criticize them.

The organizational problem

In many organizations staff appraisals are not taken seriously. They are used as a window dressing exercise and by providing comfort to top management in feeling 'we also do it'. Some managers see staff appraisals as falling outside their function and some consider them to be 'distractions'. Appraisals are often cut short because of crises or lack of time.

The communication problem

There is a lack of communication as to the purpose and the objectives of staff appraisals. For example, in one company I came across, one manager was using staff appraisals to determine the annual salary increase and merit reward whereas in the same organization another manager was using appraisals to develop his staff. There is inconsistency of purpose because of the lack of communication. There is also the problem that those who have to act as appraisers in many instances have not been trained to appraise.

The key problems associated with staff appraisals are:

- Takes longer than expected to implement.
- Inconsistency of objectives.

130

- ■ Inadequate communication
- ■ Management is distracted.
- ■ Managers do not see it as their part of their job.
- ■ Inadequate training.
- ■ Mistrust.
- ■ Inadequate interviewing technique.
- ■ Lack of 'rapport' between parties involved.
- ■ Ambiguous indicators.
- ■ Change of management/personnel.
- ■ Uncertainty.
- ■ Too much emphasis on financial variances.
- ■ Used to 'punish' rather than 'motivate'.
- ■ Often not aligned to corporate objectives.
- ■ Culture of not paying attention to 'soft' issues.

How to design performance appraisals – the people dimension

Staff should establish performance goals for themselves. Ask them to think about their job and categorize their work under about six key results areas (KRAs). These KRAs could be categorized as financial, operational, behaviour, quality-related and customer satisfaction, and others added according to the nature of the organization and the job involved. Managers should act as facilitators and give as much support as is needed at a preliminary stage.

It is always useful to ask the staff to do SWOT (strengths, weaknesses, opportunities, and threats or challenges) analysis of themselves in relation to the job they are doing and the department or teams they work in. The strengths would include information on their competencies, skills, experience, adaptability, inter-personal skills, etc. Weaknesses could relate to skills, experience, speed of adaptation, level of commitment, etc. Opportunities would encompass becoming process leader or team leader, change 'champions', facilitator, etc. and the threats would involve considering the possibility of de-skilling, moving into different areas, working with different colleagues, etc.

The approach is to sit with a subordinate and do a job map. This would involve identifying the activities, tasks, functions and responsibilities of a subordinate. The procedure would follow the framework below:

Management Ideas

I have responsibility for achieving:

....
....
....
....

My function is (to lead, to produce) to:

....
....
....

I have to perform the following tasks to meet my objectives:

....
....
....
....
....

These tasks involve the following activities:

....
....
....
....
....
....
....
....

The next stage is to sit with each member of staff and go over the objectives set for him or her. At this stage it should be clear what is expected of them and by when. The objectives set should be sensible, measurable, attainable, realistic, and have a time scale (SMART).

After the objectives have been explained and finalized, a manager should communicate expectations (outcomes desired). Before the formal appraisal is done, a manager should monitor progress according to what has been agreed and provide coaching and counselling.

At the appraisal interview it is very important that the manager has done his or her 'homework' on the appraisee and has all the information ready. The focus at the appraisal should be on analysis in order to enable an appraisee to become an active participant in the process. It is important that the right basis is established for a constructive climate and action. Communication should be open and honest.

The feedback given should address the following questions on behalf of the appraisee:

- What is expected of me?
- How am I doing?
- How can I improve?
- What is my reward?
- Where do I go from here?

Finally the appraisal should be written recommending development action to be taken and most importantly how and when and by whom the action should be implemented.

The appraisal cycle should be iterative (Figure 6.5).

Figure 6.5 The performance appraisal cycle

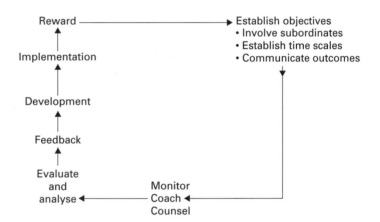

The 360-degree feedback method: are you ready for it?

Quite a lot nowadays is said about the 360-degree feedback method. Essentially this method of feedback focuses on receiving appraisals from colleagues, a manager, and the people with whom one comes in contact in normal business. Performance appraisal becomes the result of feedback received from various sources (Figure 6.6).

The information is usually collected through questionnaires. The feedback is given anonymously.

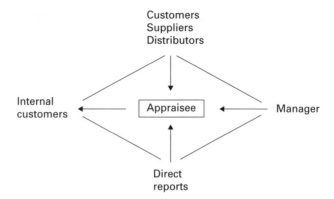

Figure 6.6 360-degree feedback

Usefulness of the method

- The feedback is comprehensive.
- It enables the individual to enhance his/her SWOT analysis.
- It is balanced feedback, taking all the stakeholders into consideration.
- It could be used at any level.
- It appears fair.
- It describes behaviour rather than passing judgement.
- It is a good way of assessing how you see yourself and how others see you
- It is meaningful.

Critical success factors of 360-degree feedback

- It must be thought out very carefully before it is implemented.
- Some organizations introduce such methods as a window dressing exercise.
- The philosophy and objectives of the system need to be understood throughout the organization.
- Those conducting appraisals have to be trained in interpreting behaviour indicators and communicating such indicators.
- There has to be a culture of trust in the organization.
- The system should focus not only on task performance but also on 'relationship' indicators.

■ There should be a consensus on core values and an alignment of individual and corporate values.
■ Action plans should focus on improvements and enhancement of core competencies.

Self appraisal – personal SWOT analysis

in brief

"I often marvel that while each man loves himself more than anyone else, he sets less value on his own estimate than on the opinions of others."
Unknown

Many organizations are embarking upon self-assessment to drive continuous improvement. It is considered to be a very effective way for organizations like ICL, Kodak, Miliken, TSB and others to get a clear picture of their organization's performance. Similarly I believe self-assessment for individuals should also be undertaken to drive continuous improvement at a personal level.

Employees work under considerable pressures, especially within the context of downsizing and restructuring, and in a constantly changing business and work environment. Apart from assessing their strengths and weaknesses formally they also have to assess how they are managing their time and stress at work. Time mismanagement is a key contributing factor to personal inefficiency and stress. How often do we hear 'If only I had time' or 'I wish there were more than twenty-four hours in a day.'? If there were it would still not make any difference if you were not conducting self assessment. Do, therefore, pay attention to your time and stress level.

ACTION

How do you rate as an employee?

Scoring: Give 1 point for 'Yes' and 2 points for 'No'.

1.	I know the mission of my organization.	Yes/No.
2.	I agree with the vision statement of my organization.	Yes/No.
3.	I understand the relationship between my department's objectives and our corporate objectives.	Yes/No.
4.	I have full information on what my company wants to do.	Yes/No.
5.	I have read the financial reports of my company.	Yes/No.
6.	I ask for explanation if I do not understand the accounts.	Yes/No.
7.	I like working in teams.	Yes/No.
8.	I like sharing information with my colleagues.	Yes/No.
9.	I like assessing my own performance.	Yes/No.
10.	I can take constructive criticism.	Yes/No.
11.	I understand the nature of the project I am working on.	Yes/No.
12.	I share my feelings with my close associates.	Yes/No.
13.	I prioritize my activities.	Yes/No.
14.	I plan my daily work.	Yes/No.
15.	I do not take my work worries home.	Yes/No.
16.	I like to acquire new skills if needed.	Yes/No.
17.	I am willing to change my job within the company, if necessary.	Yes/No.
18.	I like to be involved in discussing my own targets.	Yes/No.
19.	I do say 'no' if I cannot cope.	Yes/No.
20.	I do help my colleagues if I can.	Yes/No.
21.	I do allow time for relaxation.	Yes/No.
22.	I do believe in delivering service excellence.	Yes/No.
23.	I treat my colleagues as my customers.	Yes/No.
24.	I always look for an opportunity to acquire a new skill.	Yes/No.

24 points. You are an excellent employee.
24–28 points. You are an OK employee.
29–36 points. You have to make an effort to improve.
37–48 points. You have to make a lot of effort to improve.

Selected reading

The Economist Intelligence Unit Report (1994) The New Look of Corporate Performance Measurement.

The Open University Business School Course B889: Performance Measurement and Evaluation.

Richard Lynch and Kelvin F. Cross (1991) *Measure Up*. Basil Blackwell.

Walter Reid and D. R. Myddleton (1988) *The Meaning of Company Accounts*. Gower.

Martin Scott (1992) *Time Management*. Century.

7 Empowerment

"You can't light a fire with a wet match."
Texan saying

in brief

Summary

■ Empowerment is another management phenomenon of the 1980s and 1990s.
■ It is about getting the best out of people.
■ Karl Marx and empowerment: the concept of alienation.
■ Empowerment and motivation: Maslow, Herzberg and McGregor.
■ Is empowerment the same as delegation?
■ Delegation and how to do it: some guidelines.
■ Barriers to delegation.
■ Empowerment: its nature and essence.
■ The empowerment plan.
■ Empowerment at Miliken.
■ Empowerment and organizational change: Digital Equipment Co. case study.
■ Key success factors.

Power to the people

Empowerment became one of the key management buzz words in the early 1990s. Whether you talk about instituting total quality management, benchmarking, re-engineering or performance management you come across the concept of empowering people. Companies like Motorola, AT&T, Rank

Empowerment

Xerox, ICL, BP and Miliken have all improved their business performance by empowering their people.

Empowerment is about people. In most recent times the most influential 'guru' who has focused senior management's attention on people within the organizations has been Professor Rosabeth Moss Kanter. In her book *The Change Masters – Corporate Entrepreneurs at Work* which was published in 1983, she emphasized the need for people in organizations to work as 'corporate entrepreneurs'. The top management should learn to 'trust' their people and give them power to be innovative and bring about changes. In one of her chapters, entitled 'Empowerment', she gives examples of various situations in which people have played key roles in making organizations be adaptive to market needs.

Since then other management gurus like Tom Peters, Richard Pascale and Robert Waterman have highlighted the importance of empowering people to bring about business renewal.

The focus on people is not a new concept. It has been with us for over a century now. So how does the present focus on people in terms of empowerment differ from what has been happening in the past? Let us first look at the nature of the focus on people in the past and distinguish it from the concept of empowerment.

Focus on people – views from early gurus

For a very long time (almost 150 years), focus on workers was put on as a complement to the machine. Adam Smith in the second half of the eighteenth century had put forward his theory on the division of labour and, as we have seen, many factories adopted his preaching on specialization.

Then came F. W. Taylor who put forward his *Principles of Scientific Management* (1911). He advocated his system to maximize 'prosperity' for employers and workers. Workers would benefit by earning higher wages and by working efficiently. He advocated the development of a true science

Management Ideas

of work, the scientific selection and progressive development of the workman, the constant co-operation of management and man.

Karl Marx was concerned about the 'modern' production method which removed from men control over their work to the extent they failed to be involved in it. In Marx's view technology and division of labour resulted in the alienation of workers from their work. This alienation had three aspects: powerlessness (workers have little control), meaninglessness (workers cannot relate their work to whole production) and isolation (workers cannot form part of the production system). Alienation could result in widespread degradation and suffering.

Marx's idea was supported my many intellectuals in the 1840s. They felt the new method of working was detrimental to the workers' self-image and creativity. The theory of alienation in industry contained basic insights into the effects of sociotechnical systems on human satisfaction.

It was not until beginning of this century that the focus shifted from attention to the worker as a complement to the machine to attention to the worker as an individual within a group.

All students of management have come across the Hawthorne investigations. Elton Mayo, professor of industrial research in the Graduate School of Business Administration at Harvard University, conducted investigations at the Hawthorne Works of the Western Electric Company in Chicago during the period 1927–1932.

The investigations concluded that the favourable changes in productivity gains were attributed to an increase in work satisfaction due to freedom in the working environment and control over their own pace of work. The workers and supervisors developed a sense of participation and pride. These investigations led to the understanding of the 'human factor' in work situations.

In 1943 Abraham Maslow put forward a theory of motivation in the form of a hierarchy of needs. Human needs have certain priorities and each level must be satisfied to some extent before the next becomes dominant. The basic needs and their priority as established by Maslow are:

■ Physiological needs.
■ Safety needs.

Empowerment

- Social needs.
- Esteem or ego needs.
- Self-actualization needs.

According to the needs concept, management has the task of rearranging organizational conditions and structures in order to enable workers to achieve their own goals best by directing their own efforts toward the objectives of the organization.

In the late 1950s Professor Frederick Herzberg and some of his colleagues conducted research into work and motivation. The initial investigation was carried out among engineers and accountants and the results were published in the book *The Motivation to Work*.

The study showed that factors which contributed to job satisfaction were different in kind from those which contributed to job dissatisfaction. Job satisfaction was due to the following factors:

- Achievement.
- Recognition.
- Attraction of the work itself.
- Responsibility.
- Advancement.

Job dissatisfaction on the other hand was due to the following factors:

- Company policy.
- Supervision.
- Salary.
- Inter-personal relations.
- Working conditions.

This motivation–hygiene theory has shown the inadequacy of previous management assumptions about workers' motivation. Both Herzberg and Maslow have shown that the higher level needs cannot be met unless the characteristics of tasks are changed and workers are given the opportunity for autonomy. Herzberg's theory has also led to the suggestion of 'job enrichment' – the designing of the job to incorporate aspects which provide the opportunity for the employee's psychological growth.

Management Ideas

In 1960 Douglas McGregor published a book *The Human Side of Enterprise* in which he put forward his proposition that the traditional command and control management style implies basic assumptions about human motivation which he characterized as Theory X. These assumptions are:

- The average human being has an inherent dislike of work and will avoid it if he can.
- Because of this they must be coerced, controlled, directed and threatened to get them to make an effort.
- The average human being prefers to be directed and wishes to avoid responsibility.

He proposed Theory Y with the following assumptions:

- Work is as natural as play or rest.
- External control is not the only means of obtaining efforts.
- The most significant reward that can be offered in order to obtain commitment is the satisfaction of the individual's self-actualization needs.
- The average human being learns, under proper conditions, not only to accept but to seek responsibility.
- Many more people are able to contribute creatively to the resolution of organizational problems than do so.
- At present the potentialities of the average person are not being fully used.

McGregor advocated making work meaningful and creating 'supportive relationships'.

McClelland in 1961 and Atkinson in 1964 emphasized the need for achievement, affiliation, power and autonomy. They believed that these needs remain 'latent' until activated by environment, when they become 'manifest'.

In the 1960s considerable emphasis was put on delegation in order to manage the span of control. Delegation was also advocated to improve the quality of life.

Delegation

Division of labour created a hierarchy of command. Line authority relationships came into being as a result of vertical or scalar growth of the organization. Authority in such a structure flows downward in the organization and acceptability flows upwards. Managers rely upon delegating authority to free themselves for more important activities. But managers must bear the full responsibility for their subordinates and take the blame for wrong decisions.

The Oxford Dictionary defines delegation as 'entrusting of authority to a deputy'. In management terms delegation implies breaking down responsibility into tasks; analysing tasks to measure whether they are suitable for being carried out by specific individuals and assessing individuals to see whether they are suitable for carrying out these tasks in terms of ability, motivation and time available.

The following guidelines used to be provided for delegation:

■ Consider the 'responsibility' which you wish to delegate.
■ Analyse the responsibility in terms of separate tasks and write these down.
■ Write down which of these tasks can be delegated and which have to be done by you.
■ List those which have to be done by you and decide their order of importance and priority.
■ Set a timescale for yourself for completion of your own tasks.
■ List the individuals to whom you could delegate tasks.
■ Rate their suitability for carrying out some or all of the tasks in terms of (a) capability and experience, (b) availability, (c) motivation and (d) other factors which may affect them.
■ Select the right candidates in terms of the above rating and urgency of tasks.
■ Counsel the appropriate individual to ascertain: (a) whether he/she is capable or experienced enough, (b) whether they are available and (c) whether they are willing to do the work.

If he/she is not experienced but capable, decide whether they can be coached or trained within the timescale. If he/she is not motivated, but capable and/or experienced, then you will have to think about and initiate 'negotiation' to persuade them to accept responsibility without intimidation. If the individual is not available or restricted from doing the work, consider whether this obstacle could be overcome; if the answer is positive, the problem is avoided. If negative, move on to the most likely candidate.

Delegate work by explaining the details of 'active listening' to make sure that the facts are clearly understood. Set a timescale and arrange intermediary time for checking progress, if necessary.

Barriers to delegation

Barriers in the delegator:

- I like doing it myself.
- I can do it better myself.
- I can't explain what I want.
- I don't want to develop subordinates.
- Insecurity.
- Perfectionism: I can't tolerate mistakes.
- No time.
- Envy of subordinate ability.
- More comfortable 'doing' rather than 'managing'.
- Lack of organizational skill.
- Failure to follow up: people do what we *in*spect not what we *ex*pect.

Barriers in the delegatees:

- Lack of experience.
- Work over-load.
- Avoidance of responsibility.

Barriers in the situation:

- Boss won't tolerate mistakes.
- Decisions are too critical.
- No one to delegate to.
- Urgency.
- Under-staffing.
- Responsibility/authority position not clear.

Are you delegating properly?

■ Do you leave your work with further tasks to do at home?
■ Do you have to keep close tabs on the subordinate who is doing the job in order to exercise control?
■ Do you spend more time getting the job done yourself than spending time planning and managing?
■ Do subordinates bring all their problems to you instead of making decisions themselves?

If the answer to some or all of the above is 'yes' then you have to learn to delegate.

Practicality should be the guiding principle in delegation. A manager who does not delegate has less time to interact with his colleagues. Delegation enables development of subordinates' capability, builds their confidence and enriches their work.

Delegation and the principles of delegation are very important in many organizations today. Not all organizations are ready to empower their workers and some confuse themselves between delegation and empowerment.

What is empowerment?

Empowerment is defined as the act of releasing human energy. It is about creating situations where workers share power and assume the responsibility of making decisions for the benefit of the organization and themselves.

To use the motivational perspective, it is about providing an opportunity to gain achievement, responsibility and advancement and it is also about eliminating meaninglessness, powerlessness and isolation.

It is, however, different from motivation in that empowerment happens in a different context. Success in the marketplace depends not only on the quality of top management decisions but also on their effective implementation throughout the workplace. Survival and reward go to those businesses which can develop and sustain the commitment of the whole workforce and maintain people's capacity for continuous change.

Management Ideas

Those who advocate empowerment argue that in the delayered organizations where teams operate, it is important to:

- give people power to make quick decisions;
- get people's commitment and involvement;
- enable people to determine their own destiny;
- release into the organization the power that people already have to make decisions.

We have seen in total quality management, delivering service excellence and business process re-engineering, that quick responses to customers' needs is important and the only way one could manage effectively in a delayered structure is to empower employees. As Mark Brown, an independent consultant and the author of *The Dinosaur Strain* puts it 'to empower people is to enable them to be the "customer within".'

Empowerment is different from delegation because it takes place within a different organizational structure and in a situation where work is done in teams. Delegation takes place in a hierarchical organizational structure. Secondly, in delegation, an aspect of the manager's responsibility is 'given' to the subordinate, whereas in empowerment there is dispersal of power throughout the organization.

Empowerment is based on the assumptions that:

- Employees want responsibility.
- They want to own a problem.
- They are all rational.
- They understand the corporate mission and goal.
- They feel they are trusted.

Empowerment is central to the renewal of corporation. Over the years people down the line have come up with very creative and effective solutions to help organizational renewal. Robert Waterman in his book *The Renewal Factor* cites stories of the *Wall Street Journal* and Delta Airlines where employee participation played a significant role in corporate renewal.

However, in empowerment trust plays a very important role. Management guru Richard Pascale believes that values and trust are pre-conditions of empowerment. These two factors encourage individuals to think, experiment and improve. Empowerment transforms commitment into contribution.

In the book *Transforming Corporate Culture* by David Drennan, the following two stories illustrate the pay-off of trust. The first story relates to Marcus Sieff of Marks & Spencer.

Sieff believed that the company was awash with duplicated paperwork, and that much of it could be eliminated by trusting employees to do a good job and to use common sense in solving day-to-day problems. He started with a team to examine the company's paperwork to see what could be cut out. They had some early successes; for example, the first experiment cut out six million pieces of paper a year. He still felt they had to do something dramatic to get the message across.

At the time, stock-rooms in each store were protected by walls, and sales staff had religiously to complete stock-order forms to get stock-room staff eventually to bring down the goods they wanted to their counters. Sieff decided at a stroke that sales staff should be able to go and fetch their own stock direct from the stock-rooms. The chief accountant protested that there would be a huge increase in stealing, but Sieff went ahead anyway: he believed most people could be trusted. In the end, the level of stock was no greater than before, but in the process they eliminated some 26 million forms and documents, sold off 1000 filing cabinets they did not need any more, and 1000 stock-room assistants were able to be transferred to the sales floor. At the same time Sieff reinforced his trust in his people by getting rid of several hundred time clocks and punctuality actually improved.

Do you think the message got round the company? Without doubt it did. People may hear you spouting about simplification and trusting employees, but they are never quite sure whether you mean it, especially if they have a boss like the chief accountant.

The other story in the book relates to what Rene McPherson did at Dana Corporation in the USA. 'Almost every executive agrees that people are their most important asset, he said, 'yet almost none really lives it'.

When he took over as chairman he felt the company was far too bureaucratic and centrally controlled, effectively stifling

people's initiative and ideas. When he piled the corporate policy manuals on top of one another they measured over 22 inches! He threw them all out and replaced them with a one-page policy statement. Said a vice president: 'We have no corporate procedures at Dana. We threw the books away. We eliminated reports and sign-offs. We installed trust.' That trust showed in reducing corporate staff from 600 to 100, leaving factory managers alone to mind their own 'store' and do their own buying without interference, and, as McPherson said, 'turning the company back over to people who do the work'.

Source: Transforming Company Culture **by David Drennan (1992) McGraw-Hill.**

Empowerment does not happen by issuing memos. A chief executive officer of one organization stood up at a meeting and announced to those present, 'Guys you are now empowered. Be creative and make decisions as long as you inform your bosses and conform to the rules of the organization'. As far as new management thinking is concerned, this particular chief executive officer feels he is 'with it'.

In an article entitled Navigating the Journey to Empowerment by W. Alan Randolph which appeared in *Organizational Dynamics*, Spring 1995, the author presents the following plan for implementing empowerment:

The empowerment plan

Share information

- Share company performance information.
- Help people understand the business.
- Build trust through sharing sensitive information.
- Create self-monitoring possibilities.

Create autonomy through structure

- Create a clear vision and clarify the little pictures.
- Clarify goals and roles collaboratively.

Empowerment

- Create new decision-making rules that support empowerment.
- Establish new empowering performance management processes.
- Use heavy doses of training.

Let teams become the hierarchy

- Provide direction and training for new skills.
- Provide encouragement and support for change.
- Gradually have managers let go of control.
- Work through the leadership vacuum stage.
- Acknowledge the fear factor.

Remember: Empowerment is not magic; it consists of few simple steps and a lot of persistence.

Reprinted, by permission of the publisher, from *Organizational Dynamics*, Spring 1995 © 1995. American Management Association, New York. All rights reserved.

Many senior managers are afraid to empower their staff. Some of these managers have spent a number of years gaining power, so giving it away is a very difficult thing to do. The problem is that power is viewed as a fixed sum. If I give you some of my power that means I have less power. There is a lack of dynamics of power. Empowering people increases the total power within the organization as most of the people already have power to make decisions but not the opportunity. Empowerment provides that opportunity.

Richard Newton, head of HR at BP Co., highlighted the following basic rules of empowerment at a conference on empowerment organized by the Economist Conferences:

1. Articulate clearly and openly the company's business goals.
2. Align individual aspirations with those of the company.
3. Reconcile career and personal objectives with business goals.
4. Recognize and encourage business flexibility or diversity.
5. Establish effective global linkages to achieve group synergy.

Management Ideas

At the same conference William Guitink, vice president for management training and development at Philips Electronics BV, explained an approach to the transformation of Philips. He said that revitalization at Philips is about enlisting the energies and talents of all the people to bring about lasting change. The road to successful change and sustained profitability consisted of a number of steps which he highlighted under the headings of:

- Creating a shared mindset.
- Changing behaviour.
- Building competences/capabilities.
- Improving business performance.

Empowerment can be looked at from an organizational perspective and an individual perspective. Organizations can empower by creating an appropriate climate and good leadership to facilitate. Employees have to be convinced that top management mean business and that they have trust in their employees. However, at the end of the day it is people who have to empower themselves. They have to give commitment and involvement. This is the nature of the 'psychological contract' these days. The way businesses are going and have gone employees feel very insecure and have less or no loyalty. If the promotional ladder has disappeared in order to get workers to be flexible and adaptive to change, then present employees expect 'modern' organizations to create a climate for them to be creative, use their heads and be treated with respect. Empowerment provides that opportunity.

At the conference mentioned above, Alastair Wright, former director of human resources at Digital Equipment Co., emphasized the fact that organizations are designed to disempower. Only the empowered can empower. People must empower themselves and this must come from within.

If organizations do not empower their people they will not be able to recruit and retain people who can help them survive in the changing profile of the business world. As far back as 1970, when some organizations were having problems recruiting good graduates, a survey was conducted asking one in four male undergraduates why the UK industry was not able to recruit its full share of graduates.

Among the reasons given were:

- Lack of sufficient opportunity to be creative.
- Loss of individual identities.
- Involvement in a 'rat race' within the organizations.

This was twenty-five years ago. In the 1990s if the employers do not make a 'new deal' with their people they will face very acute recruitment and staff turnover problems.

Recently the author conducted a word association exercise in relation to the concept of empowerment with a group of business executives. The following words kept on creeping up:

- enthusiasm
- enabler
- creative
- intellectual
- human being
- energetic
- decision-making
- authority
- respect
- pride
- fulfilment
- values
- responsibility
- influence
- achievement
- confidence
- trust
- commitment
- loyalty
- employability
- initiative

These words provide us with an insight into the concept of empowerment and should enable us to distinguish it from worker participation or delegation.

Organizational desperation or genuine desire to experiment?

In various organizations today the most amazing things are happening. Dr Steven Covey is making his mark on many organizations. His best-selling book, *The Seven Habits of Highly Effective People*, is about moral renewal and self help. He believes that to do good you have to be good. The focus of his teaching is on individual and organizational morality.

Management Ideas

He preaches formation of habits by doing the following:

- Individuals should take initiatives and responsibility.
- Begin any task with an end in mind.
- Put first things first. Be in control of your feelings and moods.
- Think win/win.
- Seek first to understand then to be understood.
- Synergize the situation by thinking that wholes are greater than the sum of their parts (2 + 2 = 5).
- Take time to cultivate the physical, mental, social, emotional and spiritual dimensions of yourself.

His book and his advice is addressed 'To my colleagues, empowered and empowering.'

Do businesses take him seriously? Yes. Companies like AT&T, Ford, Xerox, Dow Chemical are all serious about his advice. The organizations are beginning to search for their 'souls' with a view to maximizing the potential of their employees. Some individuals have started consultancy companies to advise organizations to search for their corporate morals.

The poet David Whyte, from Yorkshire, uses poetry to help individuals and organizations to understand creativity. Organizations are now striving to change in order to make their workers feel good about working so that they become highly motivated and involved.

People become the cornerstone of the success of many projects in which organizations get involved. At a conference on empowerment, Clive Jeanes, managing director of the European Division of Miliken Industrials Ltd, emphasized the role played by empowered employees in bringing quality success in Miliken.

There are many stories from various organizations of how some of their employees have taken initiatives to bring about corporate renewal or new products in the market. The story of 3M and 'Post-its' is very old now but it does make the point of employees' 'freedom' to be creative. 3M always believed in 'allowing' their workers to work in their own way. Empowerment in some organizations has been practised long before it became fashionable management thinking.

Empowerment is important now for all organizations, mainly because of the intensive changes taking place in the marketplace. Yes, it has been practised in some organizations for a number of years, but what is important is that it should be practised by all organizations who want to survive in business and it is also very important that the concept is understood properly. Empowerment should not be an exception in the philosophy of managing people in the 1990s or in the twenty-first century.

Empowerment through organizational transformation

Does empowerment work through organizational change? To answer this question is to examine the case of Digital Equipment Co. This case study illustrates **how empowerment can be maintained through organizational change**. It is the case study of restructuring in Digital as presented by David Allen-Butler of Digital Equipment Co. at one of the Economist Conferences.

Case study: Digital Equipment Co.

... In presenting Digital as a case study let me stress that I do so in the spirit of sharing with you our successes and disappointments and not as some kind of paragon with all our challenges safely behind us...

In the dictionary, empowerment is defined as 'Authorize; license; give power to; make able'. These are, however, what I would describe as a layman's definition and not adequate for the purpose of the case I present to you today. These are all words that can best be described as inputs. And I don't see empowerment as an input. I see empowerment much more as a result, an output from a system that is both complex and difficult to define.

Working in an empowering environment: 'Doing the right thing'

To understand where my argument is leading to, it's necessary to go back a few years. Digital started over thirty-six years ago, as a computer technology company of three employees headed by Ken Olsen. Ken was later to be labelled by *Time Magazine* as 'the ultimate entrepreneur'. He set up the company in August

Management Ideas

1957, in 8500 square feet of converted woollen mill in Maynard, Massachusetts. The first fiscal year saw sales hit $94, 000.

After ten years we had grown in revenue to $38m and 2500 employees. By the end of the second decade we had achieved an annual revenue of $1bn with 36 000 employees.

I joined the company in 1987, its thirtieth year. Digital had made it into Fortune's list of the top 50 US companies at number 44. Employees exceeded 120 000 and revenue was heading for $12bn. By 1989 revenue had exceeded $12.7bn. We were employing nearly 126 000 world-wide.

In 1990 we were at Fortune's number 27 position. We had become the US's second most successful company of the decade, with an annual compound growth rate of 21.7 per cent. In 1991 our revenue hit $13.9bn. Digital was number two after IBM.

. . .What was not apparent was the looming problem this growth was creating. After all, employees are our greatest asset and our biggest expense. 1990 was the year when things changed!

That's when the market took a dramatic turn. The bottom seemed to fall out of the world economy. The US IT market was devastated. Europe was beginning to follow the US. The Asia-Pacific region and Eastern Europe were still relatively undeveloped and not growing at a rate that would compensate for the drops being seen in Europe and the US. IT companies were collapsing, WANG being a painful example.

In 1992 Digital lost $2.79bn. Yes, that's nearly three billion dollars. Fortunately, that was against the backdrop of a very strong balance sheet. But no balance sheet can stand that sort of hit for long. Some of us wondered if it was coincidence that we changed the colour of the corporate logo to red at this time!

That's enough about the environment in which we were operating. Let's look at the principles on which the company was founded, and the culture that developed from them.

Ken had a unique management style. He was strongly religious and a had a fundamental belief in people. The 'founder culture' that evolved from his leadership can best be described as a valuing of the individual. Digital invested enormous amounts of time and money in the development of its employees. Ken also believed in the principles of honesty and trust. He believed that each employee would 'Do the right thing', a catch phrase that became synonymous with Digital. This philosophy worked well, and the company grew rapidly, as I've already summarized.

Empowerment

A substantial people management and human resource philosophy evolved. Digital's current (1994) corporate human resource philosophy states:

People will be energized and create a competitive advantage for the company when they:

- have a sense of purpose;
- are treated with respect, dignity and fairness;
- apply their skills to meaningful work;
- are encouraged and are able to contribute;
- have opportunities to grow;
- are able to integrate their work with the work of others;
- embrace change with confidence and openness.

However, the company was also growing more and more complex, our customers were becoming confused, our employees were becoming confused. Like most of the big IT companies, we had evolved a complex, world-wide, multi-layered, national and international sales and management structure, heavily matrixed – and that means duplication of work and effort. Everyone was 'doing their own thing'. With the wisdom of hindsight, it is clear this is *not* the same as what is meant by 'doing the right thing'. What the company lacked was a sense of purpose and a clarity of direction. Ken even stimulated competition between lines of business, putting one product line directly against another. He believed this would generate healthy competition, instead it caused infighting and inefficiency. Individual employees did not have a single context in which to operate and did not share a common vision about the future, decisions were often taken in isolation.

To help you to understand how this freedom to act played itself out I will cite a few examples. There is a project review process in Digital called the 'Phase Review Process'. Over the years it evolved into a separate process for each of the engineering groups. The result was fifteen similarly intentioned, but differing, processes within one function. Another example, in sales we have counted as many as thirty-two different forecasting processes. A more recent example of this 'diversity' is the fact that last year Digital Equipment Company Ltd made six entries in the DTI handbook. Each was sponsored and funded by a different part of the business (with different fees being negotiated), and the messages were different, even contradictory. Another example of our complexity, we discovered we had 340 000 part numbers in multiple and complex catalogues. We discovered that only 14 000 sold in quantity and the vast majority could be consolidated and rationalized.

This complexity was not just apparent within Digital. A customer needed as many as eighteen phone numbers to track down the required service.

The stock market also saw the writing on the wall. As recently as 18 April, Louis Kahoe's editorial in the *Financial Times* had the leader 'Digital Equipment losses raise question of control'. From a high of $198 in September 1988, we hit a low of $19 in April 1994.

A so-called empowering culture had created a confused, confusing and inefficient organization. What may have been right for a small growing company in more profitable times, in a growing market, was almost certainly not right for our customers, who need simplicity in their dealings with us. Operating in the highly commutative world of IT, Digital needed to change and change fast.

Centralization versus decentralization

But what does it need to change to, and how? There is a big debate raging about the benefits of centralized organizations compared to decentralized organizations. Words associated with each of these organizational types can be seen as positive or negative, depending on one's stance. Digital has experience of both, but historically seemed to favour centralization from a business and technological perspective and decentralization from an employment perspective, tailoring employment conditions to the local labour market. In the past this has worked well. In 1990, Digital UK reorganized its selling organization into what it called the entrepreneurial model. This gave the account management organization substantial autonomy. However, we did not set any parameters or guidelines. The result was a climbing headcount, increased expense base and discontinuity. A virtual anarchy existed, which is not surprising when you consider we released fifty entrepreneurs on to our unsuspecting customers! We learnt that giving freedom to act without providing rules, guidelines or parameters leads to chaos.

The appointment of Robert Palmer as president and chief executive of Digital in July 1992 created an expectation of clearer direction setting and business focus. Bob took over the reins at a time when Digital was in the middle of a major restructuring

Empowerment

of its business. This restructuring, which started in mid-1990, had the intent of returning the company to profitability.

The challenges are threefold:

- To drastically restructure and downsize the business in order to remain competitive. (Some benchmarks suggest that Digital should be half the size it currently is, for the revenue it generates.)
- To retain many of the values on which Digital was founded and the reason so many employees were attracted to Digital in the first place (we were founded as a people company and wish to retain that philosophy).
- To reset expectations and establish new standards of working for the future. (What was acceptable yesterday is no longer adequate today and will certainly be inadequate tomorrow. Continuous improvement is necessary, just to survive.)

As soon as Bob Palmer took over, he created a clarity of purpose previously lacking in the 'old order'. However, his decisiveness and need to manage the changes quickly created a potential risk: that of having everything decided centrally and creating lack of ownership for the changes by the employees. However, Bob saw the advantages of involving employees as outweighing the disadvantages, especially in these times of dramatic change. I have now arrived at the nub of my presentation.

Let us relook at Digital's HR philosophy. Employees had lost sight of any purpose we might have had. The company was still attempting to treat employees with dignity and respect but we had set an expectation over thirty years that employees had a job for life. That expectation was dashed with round after round of redundancies.

Growth potential has apparently disappeared overnight. Instead we were perceived to be removing opportunity. For example, we made 100 of 400 managers redundant in December. People were becoming isolated from each other. They were unclear about how their work related to the work of others. And if we were confused, then our customers were certainly confused.

However, we had got some of our act together. On the technological side, innovation has been a key market differentiation for Digital. We have always held a unique position in the marketplace with our proprietary technology, the VAX. This will continue with our Alpha chip – the world's first 64-bit processor and the most powerful – developed as a world-wide initiative. Our technical capability has always been a relative strength. The resetting of our technical strategy to embrace Alpha was a corporate decision implemented world-wide. But, whilst we have been driving our technological development from a central strategy, we have been less clear about other aspects of our business, especially marketing. This has caused considerable confusion with managers, employees and ultimately our customers and suppliers. The common cry from employees is 'Where is the leadership in this company?' Again with Alpha, we undertook a world-wide marketing campaign, co-ordinated centrally, but with local implementation.

Bob Palmer was implementing a new management strategy: central direction setting, establishment of ground rules and local implementation of design and delivery.

Managing through rapid change – what of empowerment now?

In the last three years, up to December 1993, Digital has reduced its world-wide population from over 126 000 employees to around 85 000. That's a 30 per cent reduction. The UK business had also reduced its size by a similar proportion from 7000 to 4300. Continuing lack of profits and a need to realign business direction meant a further world-wide cut in 1994. In the UK this meant a further 800 employees. Another 20 per cent. We had to achieve this in six months.

So, in January, it was decided rather than undertake across-the-board cuts we would re-engineer the whole of the company, in line with the new world-wide vision and a defined corporate organizational framework. But we needed to do this in a way congruent with our HR philosophy. This required leadership and participation. New territories were established by corporate management, each territory comprising a group of countries. For example, Europe's fifteen countries were reformed into five territories. Amongst other things, this involved a substantial reappraisal of the senior management structure. However, although the territory structure and organizational size were decided centrally, each of the territories was tasked with managing their own restructuring locally. This overall corporate setting, coupled with local decision-making, was a major part of the strategy for maintaining local ownership and motivation and driving the revitalization of the organization.

In the UK we adopted a restructuring approach called process re-engineering. The managing director, Chris Conway, set up a restructuring task force. This small group comprised a customer business unit manager, a process re-engineering consultant, the UK sales administration manager and myself. The company was designed from the customer back. This involved looking at the needs of the customer (we talked with customers, researched them and looked hard and long at what the market wanted and what we are offering), evaluating each internal process and how it contributed to the value chain. This is turn resulted in a major simplification of the whole organization.

But how does this relate to the empowerment of employees, you ask? All parts of the organization contributed to the discussion and were able to make suggestions about how the work could be done in a simpler way, without duplication. Over 200 people were directly involved in the re-engineering, with the vast majority of employees represented by at least one person in the design work. The direct involvement ensured that all of the 'old' organizational groups could contribute to the creation of the 'new' environment. But all this was done within a defined framework set down by the task force; the customer value chain.

... This freedom in decision-making with defined guidelines allowed us to work quickly and enabled us to exceed the corporate benchmarks for headcount reductions, in a shorter time frame.

Clear leadership, decisiveness about the business we were in – and the businesses we weren't in – clarity about what was 'negotiable' and what wasn't, and the setting of precise targets and deadlines, enabled us to involve employees in the redesign of the UK business and over-achieve our goals.

Regeneration, optimism and energy

The future brings two certainties. Business will be impacted by continuous change, and to survive, let alone grow, business will need to undertake continuous improvement.

Digital is building a new organization to address the challenges of the future, whilst doing everything it can not to create an environment where problems grow and become difficult to address. We have learnt that giving employees substantial degrees of freedom may appear to be a way of showing that the company values the human resource, but in reality this has proved to cause virtual anarchy, which ultimately has a major negative impact on a substantial number of employees. Anarchy in a business leads to chaos which in turn leads to demoralization and a sense of failure.

Management Ideas

Japan has been over quoted in the last decade, but the truth is that it underwent a major revitalization after the Second World War, radically changing the way workers approached their work. Digital has started to tackle the same problem.

Digital is designing an organization that has a single vision and purpose, that is, clearly defined, simple processes; where employees have the ability and freedom to make decisions; where continuous improvement is a way of working; where excellence in people management is a given; which is an energizing and rewarding place to work; where leadership exists at all levels in the organization.

This then takes me to my opening comments. These were that it is very difficult to define empowerment, but one thing that's clear is that we know it when we see it.

Many of you have heard the saying: 'Power corrupts and absolute power corrupts absolutely'. I would like to leave you with my version:

Empowerment makes businesses
Absolute empowerment makes businesses obsolete.

... Digital is a learning organization, and learnt a costly lesson. The future is positive, thanks to participative re-engineering and employee commitment.

A number of organizations talk about the importance of empowerment in bringing about corporate renewal and transformation in a competitive business climate. The degree of freedom, involvement and commitment depends on the type of organization and on the calibre of top management. Empowerment is guaranteed to fail if there is a lack of courage and trust from top management, and lack of conviction on the side of employees.

The three most important success factors of empowerment are ability, opportunity and motivation. For empowerment to succeed employees:

■ must be able to make a decision,
■ must have an opportunity to make a decision, and
■ must want to make a decision.

By way of example, if top management want their employees to play pianos then first they have to provide pianos (opportunity), secondly the staff have to be able to play the pianos (skill and training) and finally they have to want to play the pianos (motivation). If employees are asked to perform beyond their ability, this will result in imbalance between actual performance and expected performance which will then result in stress at work.

For empowerment to succeed it has to have SMART dimensions:

S   It has to receive full **support** from the top management.
M   Staff have to be **motivated** to 'take' power.
A   **Authority** has to be aligned to strategic direction.
R   **Responsibility** is the core component of empowerment.
T   **Trust** in individuals and teamwork is essential.

How to empower: the key success factors of empowerment

- There must be information sharing, including sensitive information.
- There should be an appropriate leadership that can facilitate empowerment.
- There is a need for team-building.
- Employees should be trained to behave as 'entrepreneurs'.
- Employees should understand the challenges facing their businesses.
- The top management should trust their employees.
- Employees in turn should give their full commitment.
- Organizational culture should 'allow' employees to make mistakes.
- Leaders should be honest and give effective performance information.
- There has to be strong leadership in order to provide structure and direction.
- It is important to establish parameters.
- Managers should assume the role of a coach and help people to achieve their goals.

- ■ Employees should make operational decisions consistent with strategic decisions.
- ■ The organization should make 'finger-pointing' obsolete. If you find a problem you own it.

Selected reading

Mark Brown (1988) *The Dinosaur Strain*. Element Books.

William C. Byham (1988) *ZAAP: The Lightning of Empowerment*. Development Dimensions International Press.

Stephen R. Covey (1992) *The Seven Habits of Highly Effective People*. Simon & Schuster.

Ed Oakley and Doug Krug (1991) *Enlightened Leadership*. Fireside.

Richard Pascale (1989) *Managing on the Edge*. Penguin Books.

Noel M. Tichy and Stratford Sherman (1994) *Control Your Destiny Or Someone Else Will*. Harper Business.

8 The horizontal organization

in brief

"A form without substance is like an egg shell without a yoke."
African saying

Summary

■ De-layering the organization has been the 'management speak' of the 1990s.
■ The hierarchical organization and functional specialism.
■ Journey from the pyramidal organization structure to the matrix structure.
■ Attributes of the horizontal organization.
■ Shaping the horizontal organization: McKinsey's consultants' views.
  – Organize around processes not tasks.
  – Minimize non-value adding activities.
  – Assign ownership of processes.
  – Link performance objectives to customer service.
  – Form teams.
  – Combine managerial and non-managerial activities.
  – Treat multiple competencies as a rule.
  – Inform and train people.
  – Maximize supplier and customer contacts.
  – Reward individual skill development and team performance.
■ The horizontal organization is the organization of the twenty-first century.

The hierarchical organization

The flat or horizontal organization is presented as the organization of the future. The traditional vertical or hierarchical organization is based on the classical approach to management. The focus of attention was on division of labour, hierarchy of authority and span of control.

Division of labour led to the grouping of key activities and allocation of roles to individuals. The hierarchy of authority was based on the degree of authority delegated at each level of management; authority is vested in the manager by the upper echelons of the organization. Span of control relates to the number of individuals reporting directly to one manager.

The organization function of management involves developing a structure by bringing together many aspects and elements of business into a structured whole. Positions of each person or group of persons are defined in the structure (Figure 8.1).

Figure 8.1 The pyramid structure

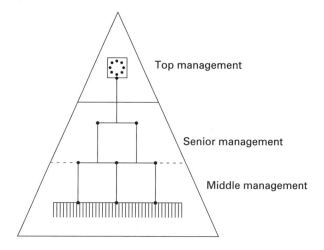

Top management

Senior management

Middle management

Hierarchy is based on a 'scalar chain of authority'. This relates to the number of levels in an organization and comes into existence whenever an individual is made the subordinate. The number of subordinates reporting directly to one manager is known as the 'span of control' and this in turn affects the shape of the organization. The larger the span of control the flatter the pyramid.

chapter 8

The horizontal organization

Some companies today are still organized around such a structure which some writers refer to as the 'command and control' model. Such a model thrived in a stable competitive environment. The basic principle of this organizational structure is that a subordinate should not report to more than one manager at a time. There must be a 'unity of command' (no conflicting demands).

Throughout history organizations had to face up to a number of issues about the kind of structure that will best sustain the success of their business. For almost a century the popular structure of the organization was based on functional specialization. Such a structure divides management into such areas as manufacturing, marketing, production and finance.

How did the hierarchical structure develop?

While the greatest management thinkers like Henri Fayol and Frederick Taylor were expounding the theories on management and organization of work, a German sociologist Max Weber (1864–1924) was formulating the concept of 'bureaucracy' which defined roles within an hierarchy where job holders were appointed on merit, and were subject to rules. According to Weber, bureaucracy is a structure based on conformity to rules, correct procedures and clearly defined jurisdictions.

As the economy developed and international trade began to grow, many businesses developed structures to suit their operations. Some structured their organizations round the product range, and others based their structure on geography.

Which structure?

Gradually as more branches and subsidiaries began to open overseas and businesses entered into the arena of mergers and acquisitions, debates evolved round the centralized structure, where all activities are controlled from the headquarters, or the decentralized structure, where subsidiaries are given some degree of autonomy while headquarters maintain senior functional managerial responsibility for corporate planning, corporate finance, company law and personnel.

Academics and consultants were constantly debating the point of the organizational structure following the corporate strategy. Structure, they say, should follow strategy. An organization should be capable of making strategic adaptation, and for this they needed structure that was not rigid. The hierarchical structure was rigid. Within such a structure rules became important in their own right; relationships became depersonalized; specialization and standardization became the norm. What was needed was a structure that was geared to task orientation.

The matrix structure

The late 1970s and early 1980s saw the development of the matrix organization. In such a structure projects are based on a cross-functional bias and employees report to their functional boss as well as to a project manager or leader. Such a structure promotes flexibility within the hierarchical structure and a good understanding of other functions and their role within the organization.

The matrix was initially developed in the aerospace industry where organizations had to be responsive to markets. Now the matrix structure is being used in a variety of organizations in the private and public sectors.

The matrix structure was the hottest innovation to hit industry since Taylor's principles of scientific management. Some critics felt that the matrix organizational structure created conflict and confusion (see Figure 8.2).

The matrix structure is useful when an organization wants to focus resources on a particular product or project. However, the matrix structure still operated within the context of the organizational pyramid. The structure, therefore, became very difficult to manage because lateral relations require special inter-personal skills and in practice some organizations found it difficult to integrate lateral processes into the vertical information flow.

Figure 8.2 Matrix management

However, the organizational pyramids prevailed and the matrix structure still operated within the pyramidal structure. Some have argued and still argue that the great pyramids of ancient Egypt have withstood the test of time. The same can be the case with the traditional structure of the twentieth century organization.

As we have seen in Chapter 1, the world of business is changing fast and dramatically. As the year 2000 approaches, the corporations leading the way will be those that not only can delight their customers but are agile enough to respond to the changing environment. To do so, processes have to be re-engineered, people have to be empowered and structures have to be adapted. Information technology will also have a radical impact both on the process and structure of organizations.

Adapting structure to meet market needs

An adaptive organization must develop a structure that will allow it to be not only reactive but also proactive. On 6 October 1995 James A. Unruh, chairman and chief executive officer of Uniys Corporation, announced 'the current Unisys matrix structure will be replaced with the streamlined decision processes, accountability and dedicated resources characteristic of stand-alone business. We will be faster and more aggressive in executing our strategy of providing technology, applying technology and servicing technology in focused markets.'

Organizations that have adopted cross-functional teams but remain too large are 'demerging' in order to be more competitive and proactive in a continually changing global business environment. AT&T stunned Wall Street in September 1995 by announcing its intention to split AT&T into three companies. The chief executive officer had taken this action at a time when the telephone and cable TV industries are about to be deregulated.

Many writers now argue that modern organizational structures are too costly, too slow to adapt and unresponsive to customer needs. Many companies are beginning to experiment with a new model of organization by de-layering the levels of the organization and working within the horizontal organizational structure. In such a structure there are no functional managers any more. Organizations have redefined their roles and responsibilities.

Instead of hierarchy of structure, organizations now create a hierarchy of teams to respond to customer and competitive needs. Such hierarchy is driven by corporate strategy to satisfy customers (see Figure 8.3).

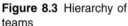

Figure 8.3 Hierarchy of teams

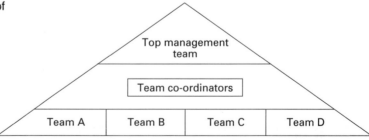

If we take the example of Royal Insurance, they have reduced ten layers to five layers of management. These are general management, senior specialists, team co-ordinators, team leaders and service providers. There has been a move from 'jobs' to 'roles'.

Attributes of the horizontal organization

Many organizations are now reducing the layers of management and adopting a horizontal structure. It is argued that this will be the shape of the organizations of the twenty-first century.

- Fewer levels of management.
- Customer-focused.
- Process-driven.
- Self-performing teams.
- No functional 'silos'.
- Effective communication.
- Faster decision-making.
- Empowerment.
- Innovative leadership.
- Work flows designed across the organization.
- Continuous performance improvement.
- Team relationships.
- Speed, simplicity and self-confidence.
- Commitment and involvement.
- The essence of the horizontal organization is the reorientation of a company around its core processes.

The horizontal organization – McKinsey's view

An ever more demanding competitive environment requires ever higher levels of corporate performance. The trouble is that needed performance improvements often remain stubbornly out of reach for companies organized in the traditional 'vertical' fashion: hierarchically-structured, functionally-oriented. By contrast, there is real performance leverage in moving toward a flatter, more horizontal mode of organization, in which cross-functional, end-to-end work flows link internal processes with the needs and capabilities of both suppliers and customers. The practical question, of course, is how to build such organizations. From the experience of many of the pioneering companies that have, at least in part,

Management Ideas

gone horizontal [the points below] distil the key design on which this alternative mode of organization depends:

1. Organize around process not task.
2. Flatten hierarchy by minimizing the subdivision of work flows and non-value-added activities.
3. Assign ownership of processes and process performance.
4. Link performance objectives and evaluation to customer satisfaction.
5. Make teams, not individuals, the principal building blocks of organization performance and design.
6. Combine managerial and non-managerial activities as often as possible.
7. Treat multiple competencies as the rule, not the exception.
8. Inform and train people on a 'just-in-time to perform' basis, not on a 'need to know' basis.
9. Maximize supplier and customer contact.
10. Reward individual skill development and team performance, not just individual performance.

Getting there from here

What will the companies be like that prove to be winning competitors in the decade ahead? There is a broad agreement on at least some of their most important characteristics: vision-driven leadership, empowered workforces, dedication to customers, total quality, and continuous improvement and innovation. Building such companies, however, will require managers to move beyond their traditional focus on functional excellence, the hallmark of the vertical organization. Instead, they will have to develop the organizational forms that leverage the cross-functional co-ordination of their own in-house activities, as well as link them closely with those of suppliers and customers.

Not surprisingly, many have become frustrated trying to create such organizations by modifying functional organizations at the margin. They have found that you can't get there from here. At either the unit level, or the entire company, you have to start in a different place – with the building blocks of the new horizontal mode of organization, which shifts the focus of organization performance from functional excellence to customer-focused improvement an innovation.

This is neither armchair theory nor airy speculation. Enough companies have moved away from their vertical past, at least in part, to convince any responsible managerial jury that significant performance gains do follow the shift to a horizontal organization. In the two years since Motorola GEG's supply management organization made the change, for example, deliveries and requisition cycle times have fallen by a factor of four, supplier quality has increased by a factor of ten, and headcount has plunged by 30 per cent. At the same time, there has been a dramatic growth in a wide variety of both individual and team-based skills. These results are not unique. Kodak, IDS, General Electric, Knight Ridder, and others have had much the same kind of experience.

As we noted at the outset, we are not arguing for the wholesale replacement of vertical organizations by horizontal ones. Indeed, neither a purely horizontal nor a purely vertical approach will serve any company perfectly. Each company must find its own proper mixture of horizontal and vertical design; balance is the key.

But finding the right balance will take careful experimentation and adjustment and tinkering. There are no certain rules or formulas. Still, the ten design principles outlined above have been widely enough tested and often enough applied that managers can confidently give them a try. They are not 'the' answer. But they are a reliable place to begin.

Reprinted by special permission from Frank Ostroff and Douglas Smith, 'The Horizontal Organization', *The McKinsey Quarterly* 1992 Number 1. © 1992 McKinsey and Company. All rights reserved. Edited version.

The McKinsey article highlights the following key aspects:

- The traditional vertical organizations lack co-ordination across tasks, departments and functions.
- Each organization must seek its own unique balance of vertical-horizontal design.
- Organizing around processes can produce performance gains.
- Many organizations like Xerox, Motorola, General Electric and Kodak are beginning to organize around horizontal, end-to-end work flows.
- The basic organization module remains a team-based work flow, not an individual task.
- Front-line teams are charged with executing all the tasks and decision-making.

Management Ideas

- Each team should 'own' each core process and be responsible for its meeting performance objectives.
- There should be an open communication throughout the work flow.
- Horizontal performance measures focus on customer satisfaction.
- Horizontal organizations combine managerial and non-managerial activities as much as possible.
- The horizontal approach encourages companies to bring their employees into direct, regular contact with suppliers and customers.

The McKinsey article, which was written in 1992, was a classical article on the nature and the benefits of the horizontal organization. Many companies took on board the principles articulated to build the horizontal organization. However, as the article says, this is not the question of either/or design.

The article comprehensively deals with various dimensions of the horizontal organization and it lays the guidelines for organizations wanting to restructure their businesses. In advocating the team approach, the article argues for the integration of processes and core disciplines.

The horizontal organization is the structure of the twenty-first century. It is the home of the 'knowledge worker'. For the next few years most organizations will be moving toward a hybrid structure but in the long run the horizontal organization will be a business reality because customers experience a company horizontally and not vertically. When a customer, for example, buys a forecasting report from the Economist Intelligence Unit, he or she does not consider going through the order department, production department, fulfilment department, invoicing or finance department. The customer orders a report and he or she expects to receive it from the company as an integrated whole.

Competitive strength in the 1990s is derived from the knowledge, skills, speed, quality and service levels provided to the customers. Companies who still stick to the command and control structure and principles (and there are some) will be the dinosaurs of the twentieth century.

Beware of causing damage

However, there is a danger of becoming too enthusiastic about flattening the structure completely. Organizations will need at least three layers in order to be managed on behalf of the all stakeholders unless of course, it was an entrepreneurial organization owned by an individual or group of individuals.

Secondly to flatten the structure effectively the organization has to invest heavily in information technology to underpin its strategy and operational activities, train all its employees to make key decisions, and constantly update its core capabilities to respond to market needs.

In early 1990 one of the big oil companies appointed a dynamic chief executive officer who was passionate about the horizontal organization. As soon as he was appointed he formulated his strategy and issued memos to all his employees informing them the organization structure will be flattened and that there will be a need to make thousands of workers redundant. Those who remain will have to work in teams and make decisions to meet customers' needs.

The employee development department was created within the human resource function to plan training for the empowered employees. Unfortunately such a decision created a lot of uncertainty and many key employees left the company. Effectiveness of employees who remained in the company decreased because they found it difficult to cope with their new roles and training for the new roles at the same time. Eventually the business as whole began to suffer but the chief executive officer was confident this was only a temporary situation and the performance would improve once change initiatives begin to settle down. However, various stakeholders and the majority of the board members began to feel so nervous that they lacked the courage to persevere with their chief executive officer. The chief executive officer was asked to leave the company.

Flattening the organization requires a strategy that incorporates advanced planning as far as training and teaming are concerned and enlightened and tolerant leadership to manage the transition and the anxiety of various stakeholders.

Selected reading

Steven F. Dichter (1991) *The Organization of the 90s. The McKinsey Quarterly*, No. 1.

Robert Duncan (1979) What is the Right Organization Structure? *Organizational Dynamics*, Winter.

G. S. Hanson and Christopher Meyer (1994) Horizontal Management. *Mercer Management Journal*, No. 3.

Frank Ostroff and Douglas Smith (1992) The Horizontal Organization. *The McKinsey Quarterly*, No.1.

Tom Peters (1992) *Liberation Management.* Macmillan, London.

9 The learning organization

in brief

"If you think knowledge is expensive, try ignorance."
Unknown

in brief

"To feed a man for a day give him a fish; but to feed him for life teach him how to fish."
Old saying

Summary

■ Why the learning organization is in vogue.
■ Peter Senge, guru of the learning organization.
■ Attributes of the learning organization.
■ Barriers to the learning organization.
■ How do organizations become learning organizations?
■ Self assessment as a route to becoming a learning organization. Case study: TSB.
■ Guide to becoming a learning organization.

Management Ideas

The learning organization is another buzzword which has crept into the field of management. Organizations, big and small, have been learning to survive for a long time. The concept of learning as such is not new, even when applied to businesses. Many academics and consultants have written articles on the learning organization for a number of years.

The learning organization guru

The person who is presented as a guru on the learning organization is Peter Senge who published a best selling book *The Fifth Disciple – The Art and Practice of the Learning Organization* (1990). Peter Senge is director of the Systems Thinking and Organizational Learning Programme at the Sloan School of Management, Massachusetts Institute of Technology.

The learning organizations, according to Senge, are places 'where people continually expand their capacity to create results they truly desire, where new and expansive patterns of thinking are nurtured, where collective aspiration is set free, and where people are continually learning how to learn together.'

The attributes of the learning organization

According to Senge:

- The concept of the learning organization is a vision.
- The learning organization is continually expanding its capacity to be creative and innovative.
- Learning has to be intrinsically motivating.
- Learning is about acquiring new knowledge and enhancing the existing knowledge.
- Learning has intellectual (thinking) and pragmatic (doing) dimensions.
- Learning requires commitment and responsibility.
- Learning is about developing core competencies.
- Open and frank communication is one of the prerequisites to learning.

Senge's theory enjoyed immense popularity. In 1995 he published another book entitled *The Fifth Discipline Fieldbook* which is a more practical guide to management. He argues that to avoid company conflict, involvement in the learning organization needs to be intense and has to go beyond a team.

As far as corporations are concerned, Senge recommends taking time out for reflection. Re-engineering and downsizing are depriving corporations of that time, as remaining workers work under pressure. But taking time out is important.

Barriers to the learning organization

Many organizations have learning disabilities. Some say learning disabilities are tragic in children, but they are fatal in organizations. These are some of the reasons why organizations are slow to learn or do not learn:

- Difficult to forget past habits.
- 'If it ain't broke don't mend it' attitude.
- Lack of recognition and awareness.
- Unable to transfer skills and experience.
- Cultural resistance – 'we do not want to do things the Japanese way'.
- It is unsettling to disturb the 'status quo'.
- The culture of 'getting it right first time'.
- Lack of resources to update core competencies.
- Lack of conviction and commitment on the part of organizations and individuals.

The concept of learning is very common and all readers are familiar with it. Babies learn as they grow. Initially most of the learning takes place through parents or families. Gradually various institutions make their contributions. Various norms are injected in individuals as they grow through life. This process is known as socialization.

Our behaviour is guided by the norms and the values of the societies we live in. As we grow older we acquire more competence to adapt ourselves to the environment. As we meet other people and travel, we observe the differences and we assimilate values and norms that fit our needs and aspirations. In most cases learning takes place as we grow up.

However, in order to realize our aspirations to become whatever we wish to become, we make a focused effort to acquire specific forms of learning. To acquire new competencies we become competitive or collaborative or dependent. This is important if we want to fulfil our aspirations. Organizations learn as they conduct their operations in the business environment. But to acquire a 'best practice' they have to go in search of best practice. Like people, they also learn in different ways. Some companies learn by being competitive, some by being collaborative, some by being dependent while others prefer to be independent.

Most organizations are habit-driven organizations. Habits are learnt but once acquired become resistant to unlearning and thus inhibit future learning. As Tom Peters often says 'The most difficult thing for many organizations is to forget old habits.'

The learning organization is an adaptive organization. It is willing to benchmark against the best practice and learn to be adaptive. It is willing to empower its employees and change the organizational structure to facilitate delivering service excellence. It has a tolerant culture to allow its employees to make mistakes and learn from them.

In practice most organizations do not have courage to allow their employees to make mistakes. Talkland, a cellular telephone company, converted losses into profits by asking employees what was going wrong. In *The Fifth Discipline*, Senge gives the example of the founder of Polaroid. The inventor of instant photography had a plaque on his office wall which read: 'A mistake is an event the full benefit of which has not yet been turned to your advantage.'

In an article in *The Times* in August 1993, Desmond Dearlove wrote 'Mistakes made at work are important in the corporate learning process.' He presents two schools of thought on management, namely 'the sweep-it-under-the-carpet school' and 'the learning organization'. These are represented in Figures 9.1 and 9.2

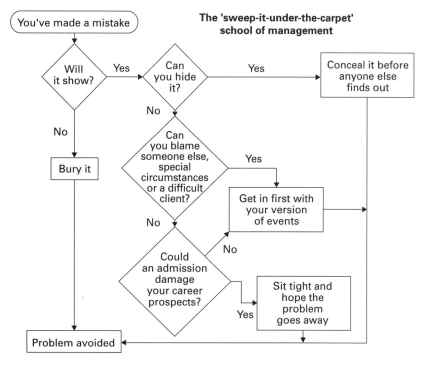

Figure 9.1 The sweep-it-under-the-carpet school of management. © Times Newspapers Ltd, 1993

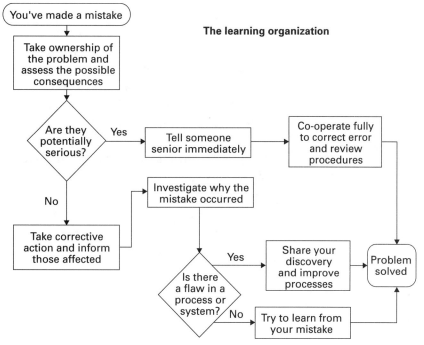

Figure 9.2 The learning organization. © Times Newspapers Ltd, 1993

How to become a learning organization

If we go behind the sweeping metaphors and grand schemes we will find that organizations adopt the following avenues in order to become creative and acquire knowledge in order to adapt to the changing environment:

- **Benchmarking**. Many organizations now benchmark their new product development process, human resource practices, marketing activities and customer service in order to adopt 'best practice'. Benchmarking has become one of the powerful tools of improving core competencies and becoming 'best in class'.
- **Total quality management**. Total quality management is one of the effective approaches to accelerate organizational learning. The Deming cycle of plan-do-check-act is a cycle of continuous learning.
- **Focus on customer service**. Re-engineering processes and de-layering organizational structure in order to be responsive to customer needs has enabled organizations to 'unlearn' old habits and become innovative and creative in managing a new way of doing business.
- **Empowerment**. Those who have truly empowered their employees and introduced a tolerant culture of facilitating entrepreneurial behaviour have become learning organizations as long as they do not get distracted from continuous learning.

To become and remain learning organizations, companies have to stick to five disciplines, namely, continuously monitor competition, benchmark to adopt best practice, have courage to adapt organizational structure, empower their employees and do not take their eyes off the customers.

Figure 9.3 The learning
organization cycle

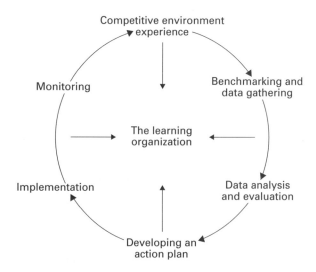

Self assessment as a route to learning

Case study: TSB

TSB is one of Britain's leading financial institutions acting in retail banking, insurance merchant banking, investment services and a number of commercial businesses. The TSB, with seven million customers, served by over 1300 branches and over 23 000 staff, is one of the best known names on the British high street.

The executive stated their commitment to total quality at the end of 1990. This was supported by the bank's mission statement and reflected in the TSB quality policy:

> We shall provide defect-free products and services to our internal and external customers which meet their agreed needs. We shall do so on time, first time and every time. Only by doing this will we achieve our mission to be the UK's leading financial retailer.

The first objective in the programme was to obtain a consistent awareness and language throughout the business. The approach used was an intensive training programme using the Philip Crosby Associates methodology. This involved a direct spend of over £7m and over 100 person years in training all staff. This exercise was completed successfully in early 1993

Management Ideas

and provided a firm foundation for other initiatives that had to be introduced to support this largest single European management development initiative.

With the training programme underway, eighteen quality improvements teams were established to represent all business areas. Each team consisted of about ten members. Their responsibility is to manage the quality improvement process for their respective business areas.

Why self assessment?

A mechanism was needed to support the quality improvement teams to ensure that the skills and knowledge acquired from the training were being applied.

Several methods of quality audit were considered, but third party assessment seemed to conflict with the 'no blame' culture encouraged by the training. Although other self assessment tools were considered, the European Quality Award model seemed to meet all requirements with the added bonus that TSB are eligible to apply for the EQA in future years.

What is our approach?

As no form of self assessment existed in TSB, it was felt that the approach must be simple and non-threatening.

The approach decided on for the first round was facilitated workshops delivered to the eighteen quality improvement teams. Manuals were produced based on the EFQM guidelines customizing the areas to address.

The workshops last one and a half days. The first session provides a background to the model: the reason for using it, an explanation of the scoring system and a self assessment of the leadership.

Individually, participants are asked to identify strengths and improvement opportunities for each of the six sub-categories and provide a score for each one. Once this is complete, individual scores are displayed on a flip chart and form the starting point for the group discussion.

The person with the highest score is asked to share their strengths with the rest of the group. These are recorded on the flip chart. After others have contributed to the list of strengths, the person with the lowest score is asked to identify some improvement opportunities and these are also recorded. This generates group discussions and gives participants the opportunity to review and change their original scores and reach a consensus score for each of the sub-criteria.

Prior to the second session, each participant undertakes a self assessment on the remaining eight categories for subsequent group discussion.

Once all categories have been covered, a prioritization process is undertaken using sticky dots. The prioritized improvement opportunities formulate the basis for an action plan. A scoring matrix was developed and is used to show the results of each team compared to the average. This will also be used to monitor progress in subsequent years.

What lessons have we learnt?

The methods used provide a good basis for the first self assessments, and, from feedback received, have proved valuable for all users. As the process was new, some of the scoring was a little subjective. They will emphasize that the scoring is not as important as identifying opportunities for continuous improvement.

Although self assessment provides the improvement opportunities to formulate an action plan, continuous improvement will only occur where the actions are implemented, monitored and regularly reviewed.

What have been the benefits?

The use of the self assessment process has provided significant benefits to the quality process within TSB. The introduction of the common framework has been effective in focusing the organizations; it has confirmed to the organization that they have only just started on the quality journey, and it has been the catalyst to developing ambitious goals for improvement in the future.

Finally, the self assessment has been effective in generating real ownership for quality amongst senior managers in the business because it forced them to examine their own activity and develop their own plans for their own areas, in their own ways.

What are our future plans?

The basic workshop method appeared to be the correct initial approach. TSB now need to develop this further in future years by moving to assessments carried out by internal teams

Management Ideas

from other parts of the business and, eventually, by preparing a written report for external assessment.

Towards the future

The group believe they have gained significant individual value from sharing between their organizations, and some themes have emerged that appear common to all companies. They believe self assessment should be an important element for any organization striving to achieve total quality.

The approach selected has to take account of the organization's maturity, its culture, its particular business environment and strategic issues. Thus what is right for one company may not be appropriate for another.

The various self assessment processes that the companies have developed and deployed in their organizations are all identifying opportunities for improvement and providing them with an effective means to prioritize them.

For greatest effectiveness self-assessment has to be positioned and introduced as an integral part of the business process and not a separate and potentially short-lived initiative.

The benchmarking framework established by the group has been a powerful tool for them and has helped them to gain maximum value from their interaction. They hope that what you have read in this short report has perhaps given you some ideas and that you can see the potential benefits of self assessment in your own organizations.

If the way the group came together seems to have been casual, well it was. The lesson they have learnt as individuals is that any such group with a common interest can start and get benefit without waiting for any external stimulus.

Source: Business Improvement through Self Assessment. European Foundation for Quality Management, EFQM Brussels Representative Office, Avenue des Pleiades 19, B-1200, Brussels, Belgium. Tel: 32 2 775 3511. Fax: 32 2 775 3535.

David A. Garvin, professor of business administration at Harvard Business School, gave an interview to *European Quality* in which he described the relationship between quality in practice and the concept of the learning organization. The article, Beyond Buzzwords – A Realistic Approach to Total Quality and the Learning Organization, appeared in Vol. 1, Number 2. A short extract is reproduced with permission of the editor, John Kelly.

Garvin on why learning is in vogue

We have shifted from an economy where the greatest asset is resources to an economy where the greatest asset is knowledge. If there is one lesson of the Japanese success story, it is that resource co-ordination has been dramatically successful in open competition. Japan is famously short of natural resources, but they succeed by adding value through knowledge: through just-in-time systems, through understanding the customer, through research, development and design. Another reason why learning is suddenly so important is that the rate of change has increased dramatically. Product cycles are much shorter. New technology has broken down the boundaries that protected industries in the past. Formerly separate industries like telecommunications and computing are now converging at great speed. All of a sudden, your knowledge base needs to be much wider and you need to assimilate new ideas much quicker than before. The landscape is changing, in some cases literally, day by day.

At the same time researchers and consultants have struggled with the vocabulary of learning. It has been really difficult to describe the process as it applies to an organization. Without doubt, 'learning organization' is one of the worst buzzwords yet devised. Its resonance is even more 'new age' and mystical than 'quality management'. It is essential to arrive at a basic definition which avoids such airy ambiguities. Stated simply, a learning organization is skilled at creating, acquiring and transferring knowledge, and at modifying its behaviour to reflect new knowledge and insights.

In order to learn, you need new ideas, otherwise you simply repeat old practices. Learning organizations are unusually skilled in problem solving, experimenting, creating, acquiring and using knowledge – as distinct from companies with data gathering resources but no processes to apply them. All too often, organizations take old practices, give them new names and end up repeating the same thing. If you gather new knowledge, but you don't change the way you work and act, you cannot consider yourself a learning organization. For example, universities are enormously skilled at creating and acquiring knowledge, but unusually cool on the idea of changing the way they act, in an administrative and business sense.

Management Ideas

Garvin on the three Ms

In the past, definitions of learning have tended to sweep past the gritty details of practice and waft about on waves of philosophy and grand themes. The trick in the learning organization is to be extremely 'nuts and bolts' about how learning is acknowledged. Apply the three Ms test to your organization: meaning, management and measurement. You can define its effectiveness and qualifications in the learning sense:

- **Meaning.** You need a plausible and clear definition of a learning organization which must be practical and easy to apply.
- **Management.** You need to put in place guidelines for practice, filled with operational advice rather than theory.
- **Measurement.** You need tools to assess an organization's rate of learning, otherwise you cannot tell whether new knowledge has been accepted and assimilated.

Once these principles are in place, the real business of learning should be rigorously encouraged. You have to adopt a systematic problem-solving approach. You cannot rely on assumptions. You need to distinguish unique events and chance occurrences from the kind of variation which requires action and is a symptom of a problem requiring a solution. Management must allow time for learning to happen. You must carefully nurture attitudes over time. But there are some obvious steps which anyone familiar with quality processes will recognize – like using brainstorming techniques, problem solving, strategic reviews, benchmarking and systems audits to stimulate knowledge gathering. Make the process of learning important, and encourage a shift away from continuous improvement towards a commitment to learning. This way, knowledge will move higher up the organizational agenda.

What is a learning company?

A learning company is an organization that facilitates the learning of all its members and continuously transforms itself. The concept is not new; it goes back to Moses. Organizations have grown from very small entrepreneurial businesses to become, over time, national and multi-national companies. Experiments have also been done including

186

changing organizational structures in order to be responsive to customer needs. Management gurus like Taylor, Galbraith, Burns, Lippit, Peters, Drucker, Argyris, Pascal, Senge, etc., have been telling us how to manage businesses in turbulent times and how to manage our business in order to beat the competition.

Every time crisis develops a 'new' piece of management thinking is born. As long as organizations do not behave like dinosaurs and are willing, with the help of their people, to become adaptive to the external environment, they can call themselves learning organizations. The key success factors are:

- All departmental or divisional activities should be aligned to corporate strategy and objectives.
- At corporate level new knowledge should be taken on board to adopt corporate strategy.

By focusing on these two aspects, the benefits are accrued at corporate level. As Senge puts it '. . .well focused actions can produce significant, enduring improvements, if they are in the right place'. Systems thinkers refer to this idea as the principle of 'leverage'.

Learning is a key aspect of the communication process. People learn by interacting with one another and by sharing knowledge and experience. The impetus for continuous learning must come from within.

Organizations learn through their people. Individuals learn through various stimuli in their environment, their experiences and their state of mind. One of the key factors inhibiting learning is the climate of de-layering, restructuring and downsizing. Even business process re-engineering has become synonymous with job cuts. According to some writers, some key companies, in undergoing corporate transformation, have caught a potentially lethal disease called 'corporate anorexia'. Such a disease has two key attributes:

- Organizations have lost the ability to be creative, which is very important in the changing competitive climate.
- Employees work in a climate of uncertainty and hence find it difficult to give their best and help their organization become a learning organization.

Management Ideas

■ Employees in such organizations have also acquired 'initiative fatigue'.

Christopher Bartlett and Sumatra Ghoshal, writing in *Sloan Management Review*, Autumn 1995, referring to the twenty large US, European and Japanese companies' experiences in transforming themselves, said, 'some companies have woken up with little to show except a massive hangover . . . Not only have the organizations become too physically strained and emotionally exhausted to maintain the momentum of improvement, but employees' day-to-day behaviour has reverted to old, familiar patterns.'

Other companies such as 3M, Intel and Kao of Japan have developed a favourable climate of entrepreneurship, collaboration and learning. According to Bartlett and Ghoshal, trust and support accompanied by discipline and stretch are the key characteristics which provide a remedy for corporate anorexia.

Learning by coaching

Another way to facilitate learning is by introducing coaching. In some organizations managers act as coaches and help their staff to improve performance and use their skills effectively. Task-oriented coaching is based on a coach showing how a particular task should be done and taking a trainee through the different procedures of completing a task. This job was undertaken by supervisors and managers.

The learning organization adopts the concept of coaching differently. A coach facilitates in bringing out the best performance from his staff. He provides an environment where the staff give their full commitment and expertise. He facilitates knowledge sharing among staff. Coaching in such organizations is developmentally based rather than being just instructional.

Again whether coaching is going to succeed or not will depend on the culture and the intention of the organization. Employees have to perceive that there is trust and commitment at the top management level. Without such a perception the learning process will be hindered.

On your way to becoming a learning organization

■ Free up information within your company. Information is knowledge.

■ Be tolerant when mistakes are made. Getting it right first time does not facilitate learning.

■ Provide resources to show commitment.

■ Do not send everyone on training courses without understanding what capabilities are required to gain and maintain competitive advantage.

■ Learning must also take place at the top. Remember we talk about a bottleneck meaning a hindrance. If you look at a bottle the neck is at the top!

■ Introduce performance measures that focus on qualitative and quantitative indicators.

■ Performance assessment or appraisal should identify and facilitate individual development.

■ Make sure that all operations throughout the organization are aligned to corporate strategy and objectives.

■ Regularly scan the environment within which your business operates.

■ Learning cannot take place without commitment and a desire to want to learn.

■ There must be an environment of continuous improvement within an organization, when asking becomes the sign of strength rather than weakness.

■ The organization has to provide self-development opportunities for all its employees.

■ Learning benefits *all* the stakeholders of the organization – top management, all employees, investors and society.

■ Finally expressing corporate vision and making patronizing statements are not enough. There has to be action throughout the organization starting from the top.

Selected reading

The American Management Association (1994) *The Learning Organization*.

John Burgoyne, Mike Pedler and Tom Boydell (1994) *Towards the Learning Company*. McGraw-Hill.

European Quality (1994) Interview with David A. Garvin, Beyond Buzzwords – A Realistic Approach to Total Quality and the Learning Organization. Vol. 1, No. 2.

Peter Senge (1990) *The Fifth Discipline*. Century.

Peter Senge (1994) *The Fifth Discipline Fieldbook*. Nicholas Brealey.

Teaming for business success

in brief

"Know how to give without hesitation, how to lose without regret, how to acquire without meanness."
George Sand

Summary

■ Many organizations now work with teams.

■ Teams go through stages of development. It is very important to understand these development stages.

■ Differences between teams and groups.

■ Factors affecting the effectiveness of teams.

■ Teams and culture.

■ Roles of teams in organizations.

■ Team performance.

■ Career development.

■ Twenty-one questions organizations must ask when forming teams.

■ Are you a good team player?

Organizational transformation

As we have seen so far in this book, organizations are under considerable pressure to improve their performance in the face of intense competition. Successful organizations are those who can respond to market needs swiftly and meet customer satisfaction. To do so has meant embarking on total quality initiatives, de-layering organizational structures, re-engineering processes, empowering employees and in some cases transforming the entire organization.

Such changes have produced many casualties and have created problems of motivation and career development. Organizations like Miliken, Rank Xerox and ICL, are continuously finding ways to leverage their employees' capabilities in order to gain and maintain competitive advantage.

In the light of all these changes many organizations have resorted to forming teams. The role of the team has become all important. Teams now form a new way of working and learning.

From groups to quality circles

In the 1960s and 1970s considerable attention was paid to the formation of groups at work. Research findings have indicated the existence of 'informal groups' and their influence on employee behaviour and productivity. Formal groups were constituted in the shape of committees and task forces to address 'ad hoc' business issues. Then came the formation of quality circles in the 1980s to improve quality and combat Japanese competition.

A quality circle consists of about five to ten volunteers who work under the supervisor, meeting once a week to identify and solve work-related problems. The growth rate of quality circles during the 1980s has been phenomenal. It is estimated that in the early 1980s there were one million quality circles and ten million members.

By the mid to late 1980s the quality circles began to lose their enthusiasm and excitement. The reasons for their failures were as follows:

- Lack of resources needed to make such groups successful.
- Some companies introduced them as a flavour of the month or as a 'quick fix'.
- Suggestions for improvements were not considered seriously by the top management.
- Supervisors or circle leaders were not trained in facilitating such groups and in group dynamics.
- People were expected to make contributions outside their work hours.

Some organizations who are cynical about teams and team-approaches to decision-making cite the examples of the failure of the quality circles without understanding that a quality circle is merely a way of doing things. What matters in the end and in practice is the way such groups are managed.

When you bring a group of people together in any situation, the important thing is to understand group dynamics. Group dynamics show how people interact in groups. At the inter-personal level, individuals have to be assured of the role they are expected to play, role conflict that may arise, status, power and group-decision making processes.

Stages of group development

Understanding the stages of group development is also important if groups (whatever they are called) have to achieve their objectives. Groups go through certain stages of development during their formation. These stages are sequential and are categorized as forming, storming, norming, and performing. Other organizational development experts have given different names to different stages and highlighted more than four developmental stages.

Forming

When people are put together at a very early stage they require guidance and direction. At this stage they are dependent on facilitators and other members and this is the stage of gathering impressions and of identifying similarities in expectations and values, and noting the differences. The focus at this stage of group formation is towards tasks to be accomplished.

Storming

At this stage competition and conflict develop. 'Oneupmanship' games are played and group members desire some structure. Questions such as 'Who is going to be responsible for what?', 'What's in it for me?', 'What are the rules and what are the rewards?' often crop up. This is the stage of the 'testing and proving' mentality.

Norming

Values get established and synchronized at this stage and group members begin to gel together and group cohesion develops. Members within the group begin to acknowledge each other's contribution and the 'let's give it a try' attitude develops. At this stage expectations, values and ideas are shared and inter-personal communication becomes effective.

Performing

The group gets into problem-solving mode and group loyalty and pride come into play. This is the most productive stage of the group formation and there is a support for experimentation. This is also the 'I'm OK, you're OK' stage.

Understanding of group developmental stages is very important. Group cohesiveness does not come into existence over-night. Many groups have been abandoned while at the storming stage. The signals from group members were misunderstood.

Teams are groups of individuals who cluster together to perform common tasks. Quality circles were specific types of teams. Charles Handy in his book *Understanding Organizations* suggests ten major purposes for which organizations use groups or teams.

1. To bring together sets of skills or talents with a view to distributing work.
2. To manage and control work.
3. For problem-solving and decision-making.
4. For processing information.
5. For getting ideas and information.
6. For testing decisions.
7. For co-ordination and liaison.
8. For increased commitment and involvement.
9. For negotiation and conflict resolution.
10. For investigation.

Attributes of teams

Many experts make a distinction between groups and teams. A **group** becomes a **team** when the following attributes are taken on board:

- There is a trust among team members.
- There is a common purpose and vision.
- Sacrifices in individuality are demanded.
- There is discipline and guidelines as to what is acceptable and what is not acceptable.
- There is a specification of goals and associated performance indicators and measures.
- There is group accountability.
- There is sharing of experience, knowledge and communication.
- There is unrestricted inter-personal communication.
- There is commitment and involvement.

These attributes give rise to 'teaming' within the groups. Teams *per se* are not important; it is the relationships and dynamics, in other words, teaming, which is important and which matters in practice.

Apart from the existence of these attributes, the effectiveness of teams depends on the structure, tasks, environment and process.

Structure

The size and composition of teams matter very much. In one recently privatized industry the top management decided to form a team of 230 people. They subsequently came to the conclusion that teams will not work in their organization. With such a number group dynamics become very difficult to manage and group developmental stages get extended. Apart from the size, the composition is very important. In order to form multi-skilled teams one telecommunications company formed teams which embraced all skills irrespective of whether these skills were appropriate to the tasks to be performed.

In other cases some skills are left out in multi-skilled teams because they may be scarce and in some cases specialists join teams at a very late stage. Again no regard is given to group dynamics.

Tasks

Teams, like organizations, have to have mission and objectives. These have to be aligned with corporate mission and strategy. It is also important to identify the nature and complexity of the tasks involved so proper direction and guidance may be provided. The leadership role in such circumstances has to change in providing coaching, supporting and training teams.

Environment

Organizational effectiveness depends on internal environment (structure, culture, management style, competencies), and external environment. Effectiveness of teams will also be influenced by external and internal environment. In a hierarchical or bureaucratic structure, teams perform less well than in an empowered climate. Equally there has to be appropriate and adequate capabilities within the teams in order to enable their organizations to be responsive to the changing external environment.

Process

Teams take time to form, storm, norm and perform. This fact is often forgotten. Whether you form multi-cultural teams or cross-functional process teams or self-managed teams, facilitating free communication, providing appropriate support and direction and motivating team members all serve to accelerate the development of effective teams.

Do not lose money on team training

In the past fifteen years and especially in the last ten years, team-building training has become a growth industry. We now have not only indoor but also outdoor training courses. These courses have some usefulness but the majority of them are a waste of money and time if the organizations have not analysed the following:

- What types of teams do we have or are we to have in the future in our organization?
- What are the team objectives?
- What skills and capabilities do we need to put together in teams?
- What is the size of the teams?
- What kind of training would they need?
- What mechanisms do we have to enable them to transfer their experience from the training field or training room to work situations?
- What role should top management play in training?

There is a tendency for many organizations to send their teams on team-building courses without seriously analysing the objectives and the pay-off.

The two other things which organizations constantly have to consider is the role of 'groupthink' which is valid in relation to teams and team maintenance. As Charles Handy said, 'Close teams can become closed teams.' Groups eventually develop their own mind and their own thinking (groupthink) and become blind to the things happening outside their groups. The role of leadership plays a key part in not allowing 'groupthink' to develop. This is done by cross-team meetings, flow of information, and the use of outsiders as catalysts. The other point to consider is team maintenance. After a while team enthusiasm may sag and it is the function of leadership to motivate and maintain the team spirit.

Teams and culture

It can be difficult forming teams and demanding team-work in societies grounded in individual values and beliefs. Very often the rapid transfers of management techniques and thinking collide with the deeply rooted mentalities of other cultures.

In forming multi-cultural teams (globalization has encouraged the formation of such teams), it is important to take some time to ponder over cultural differences that exist in social and management thinking. Being aware of different attitudes, values and beliefs will facilitate the smooth formation of teams and effective resolution of conflict at the 'storming' stage of development.

In the studies entitled *Organizational Change and Cultural Realities – Franco-American Contrasts*, the authors make the following points:

■ Americans and the French seem to favour different approaches concerning the way change should be introduced into the organization.
■ The nature of the organization is perceived very differently on either side of the Atlantic. Americans seem to perceive the organization as a system of tasks to be accomplished and objectives to be attained. French managers tend to share a personalist and social model of the organization which is perceived as a collective of persons to be managed.
■ In the American model, authority is conceived of as a way of seeing that tasks are accomplished; in the French model, activities and tasks become a prime way of establishing one's authority. Americans would ask 'who is responsible for what?' whereas the French would ask 'who has authority over whom?'.

■ The American manager perceives his role as that of a co-ordinator of resources and activities. The French manager considers it very important to have precise answers to the majority of questions he might be asked by subordinates.

In the report *Managing in Britain and Germany* (1994), published by the Anglo-German Foundation, the following are selected highlights of the differences in management behaviour and style that are relevant to teaming processes and working in teams:

■ German middle managers exhibit a more technical orientation towards their jobs, while their British colleagues stress the general management tasks of their jobs.

■ Communication of German middle managers with their subordinates is predominantly task oriented, while that of their British counterparts concentrates on motivation, reaching agreement on targets and getting policies implemented.

■ German middle managers spend more time alone than British middle managers.

■ In order to enlist support, British middle managers rely first of all on persuasion and networking. Their German counterparts trust that they can convince others primarily by the content of their arguments, not the presentation.

■ Managers in Britain and Germany hold different sets of values which give them different perspectives and lead to different ways of behaving. These value systems have an impact on motivation, satisfaction, patterns of interaction and so on.

■ The German cases studied put emphasis on *Kollegialitat* (team spirit among colleagues), *Zusammenarbeit* (co-operation, working as a part of a team) and a *gutes betriebsklima* (good working environment).

■ In Britain managers systematically took the individual as their focal point, whether responding to questions about job satisfaction, expectations of bosses and subordinates or job priorities. Typically, the British managers wanted freedom to adopt their own approach to the job; they liked work which gave them a personal sense of accomplishment and what they wanted from their bosses was recognition of their personal contribution.

Cultural dimensions

Geert Hofstede, professor of organizational anthropology and international management at the University of Limburg, The Netherlands, identified four cultural dimensions relating to different countries. These dimensions are:

- the degree of integration of individuals within the groups,
- distribution of power in society,
- uncertainty avoidance,
- differences in social roles of women versus men (endorsement of masculine or feminine qualities).

These dimensions affect the way the organizations are structured and managed. He shows how organizational practices and theories are culturally dependent.

Another person who has made his mark on the relationship between culture and organization is Fons Trompenaars, a Dutch economist and consultant. Trompenaars' research revealed seven dimensions of culture. These dimensions provide the most practical way for managers to consider how cultural differences influence their organizations and the behaviour of individuals within organizations. In every culture, he says, phenomena such as authority, bureaucracy, creativity, good fellowship and accountability are experienced in different ways. Understanding such differences will lead to effective management. Such differences are very important to consider when practising empowerment or facilitating teams. He says 'culture is like gravity: you do not experience it until you jump six feet into the air'.

Cultural diversity promotes creativity and minimizes 'groupthink'. However, forming or facilitating multi-cultural teams requires a different management style than that needed to facilitate uniform or mono-cultural teams. For example, it takes longer to establish inter-personal relationships in multi-cultural teams than in mono-cultural teams. Team leaders in multi-cultural teams have to be trained to handle prejudices, stereotyping, differences in values and attitudes and expectations.

Generally speaking, Americans adopt an instrumental approach to working in teams. The teams are there to achieve certain results, so let's get on with it. Arabs, Latin

Americans or Japanese, for example, want time to build relationships. At the 'forming' and 'storming' stages, relationship-building is more important than results.

Managing teams

The developmental stages of teaming differ in duration and management depending on whether one is dealing with mono-cultural or multi-cultural teams. The factors to consider in forming and managing teams are as follows:

- The mission and the objective of the team.
- The nature of the team and the time scale of achieving results.
- Cultural mix.
- Trust building.
- Integrity and communication.
- Development stages of team-building.
- Historical hang-ups. Previous failed attempts, for example.
- Ways of surfacing differences.
- Identifying cultural blind spots.

The role of teams in organizations

Competitive tracking

In one chemical company based in the United Kingdom, the marketing department decided to form functional teams to carry out competitor intelligence. One team was responsible for tracking financial indicators and analysing the performance of identified competitors by looking at their financial performance in relation to one specific group of stakeholders, namely, shareholders.

The other team were asked to analyse the product portfolio, product development processes and the cost of research and development. Other teams tracked customer service, labour relations and marketing and distribution channels.

These were project teams based on functions. The analysis of the competitor's performance was done in cross-functional teams and the report, incorporating an action plan, was subsequently presented to top management.

Quality

We have already examined the formation and role of quality circles. Some companies, bearing in mind the causes of failure, still work with quality circles in order to maintain the ethos of continuous improvement.

Process re-engineering

A bank, in order to re-design its branch's operations, formed multi-skilled teams to examine overall workflows and the physical layout of the branch from the customers' perspective.

In a pharmaceutical company teams consisted of a sponsor, process owner, facilitator and team members. Various teams were formed to examine the different processes required to reduce 'lab to market' time.

Teams are becoming a way of life in many businesses. Federal Express and IDS boosted productivity up to 40 per cent by adopting self-managed work teams. At Land Rover, delivery of all new products since the mid-1980s has been via project teams.

At AT&T there are four types of teams. They are quality councils, process management teams (PMTs), quality improvement team (QITs), and task teams. An improvement in the billing process, for example, will be examined by the process management team; an improvement in cycle time will be done by the quality improvement team; database improvement will be undertaken by the task team.

Project-based teams

Study a fast-moving organization like Intel and you'll see a person hired and likely assigned to a project. It changes over time, and the person's responsibilities and tasks change with it. Then the person is assigned to another project (well before the first project is finished), and them maybe to still another. These additional projects, which also evolve, require working under several team leaders, keeping different schedules, being in various places, and performing a number of different tasks. Hierarchy implodes, not because someone theorizes that it should but because under these conditions it cannot be maintained. Several workers on such teams that Tom Peters interviewed used the same phrase: 'We report to each other.'

In such a situation people no longer take their cue from a job description or a supervisor's instructions. Signals come from the changing demands of the project. Workers learn to focus their individual efforts and collective resources on the work that needs doing, changing as that changes. Managers lose their 'jobs', too, for their value can be defined only by how they facilitate the work of the project teams or how they contribute to it as a member.

Source: The End of the Job. *Fortune*, 19 September 1994.

Special tasks

Many organizations form special teams to tackle various tasks. Such teams come into existence and are then disbanded once they finish their assignments or projects.

A Japanese electronics manufacturing company constituted a special team to conduct a joint venture project with an American company. The Japanese team consisted of thirty-two members whereas the American team consisted of seven members. The teams on both sides did their homework on cultural differences and associated behaviour, as a result of which the negotiations were completed successfully. When teams of different cultures meet it is very important to balance duality: power of analysis against power of synthesis; sense of reality against imagination; rational thinking against entrepreneurship; vision against reality; action against reflection and flexibility against focus.

Team performance

Team performance needs to be measured. The right measure help teams excel. The following factors need to be considered in formulating team performance measures:

- Consistency of team objectives with corporate objectives.
- Planning of adequate resources required to do the job.
- Quality of decision-making.
- Interpersonal effectiveness.
- Sharing of information.
- Team morale.
- Levels of skills and capabilities.
- Measuring the effectiveness of the process.
- Achievement of output targets.
- How innovative has the team been?
- Assessing individual performance by peers.

Consideration for employees

The big debate over the past few years has been the reward and incentive scheme based on the team approach. There is also the question of career path. When organizations remove layers of management in order to be responsive to market conditions, they create hierarchies of teams to make the best use of the skills, knowledge and capabilities of their people. Organizational pyramids become progressively flatter. Career ladders in the traditional sense disappear and the issues of career development arise. Most of the organizations still have not come to terms with satisfying entirely their employees' aspirations when organizational structures get flattened.

When Rofey Park, a management training centre, conducted a study of flatter structures in 1994, it found that for most employees de-layering is seen as a cost-cutting exercise which results for the majority in lower morale, more work and few promotions.

Individuals are increasingly told to take responsibility for their own careers. Sony UK, for example, have a range of self development and skill-related courses which they make available to their employees. Individuals are increasingly expected to take the initiatives for themselves. We are also told by management development experts that employees are moving away from career success associated with title and status to being involved in things that give them satisfaction.

Other organizations have appointed 'mentors' whose main objective is to provide information and direction for employees to build their skills. Other organizations, by way of financial incentives, are encouraging their staff to move horizontally in order to gain long term employability. Individuals in many organizations now have to come to terms with the 'new order' and respond to the challenges of the changing business environment. People are now moving from doing jobs to performing roles. To perform various roles individuals will need to plan a portfolio of skills. Career development is about building such portfolios.

Career development – the lateral alternative

Introduction and background

Many people have heard about 3M and know a little about the company's products. There is generally less knowledge about the true breadth of the product range and the extent of the international presence of 3M.

3M has operations in fifty-eight countries, most of which are wholly owned subsidiaries of the American parent company based in St Paul, Minnesota. Some forty-two countries have their own local manufacturing facilities, very often at more than one location. In 1994 world-wide sales totalled just over $15 billion with profit after tax of over $1.3 billion. Perhaps the most unusual characteristic of 3M is the product range in excess of 66 000 items.

Quite recently *Fortune* magazine named 3M as the fifth most admired US corporation in terms of annual profits.

Organizational issues in career development

The structure of a company as large and diverse as 3M is complex and continuously evolving. Fundamentally, throughout the world, 3M businesses are grouped together into three market

Management Ideas

sectors – industrial and consumer, information and imaging, and life sciences. Each sector is organized into three or four groups which are further structured into a number of divisions.

In Europe the company has more than 18 000 employees, sales in excess of $4 billion and operations in twenty countries.

Three fundamental trends appear to be influencing the career development picture at the organizational level.

Firstly, the scope or role development is significantly increasing within the new rapidly changing and multiple networking structures, in particular at the senior professional level. Role development is achieved by extending responsibilities into broader geographic, functional or multiple business situations. When we look at job changes at middle and senior professional and management levels we see significantly more positional growth in recent times.

Secondly, we are seeing a need for greater flexibility and creativity in the way that jobs are valued within the organization. There are more requests to recognize the uniqueness of a particular role and the potential contribution of a new position. Role complexity and potential impact are seen to be more critical. This trend places significant challenge on traditional hierarchical job evaluation systems.

Thirdly, we see a structure developing that has much larger incremental steps between job levels not only as a consequence of the consolidation of management positions but also because of the tendency for role growth already described.

The overall result of these trends is to produce an organizational structure that has a significant amount of opportunity, much of it centred on developing individual expertise and as a consequence much of it unpredictable. In addition, the tendency for larger steps to develop between levels presents some challenges and real dilemmas for our development processes.

Individual issues in career development

There are no certain answers for the individual seeking career progression in today's organizations. This is probably less of a dramatic change from the reality of the past – what is different is that companies are now openly declaring that it is neither practical nor desirable to attempt to manage career development in the manner of an organizational chess game.

This apparent loss of predictability and precision in career development has many benefits for employees. There are some clear action steps that individuals can take to position themselves in the best possible situation for future opportunities, even when these are continuously evolving.

An obvious one is that of breadth of experience. Moving laterally across an organization to develop a portfolio of functional and business experience does not depend on the availability of hierarchical opportunities. People who are successful in achieving this pattern of development almost always benefit in the longer term. A broad range of experiences can be an individual's competitive edge when selection decisions are taken for tomorrow's key positions.

We encourage our people to play a full part in the human resource planning processes – performance appraisal, development planning, job information and career workshops. We sponsor networks to exchange information and share expertise and encourage cross-functional teamwork.

We also place great emphasis on individual ownership for personal development and look for a high level of commitment to both the current role and development for broader responsibilities. This aspect is reinforced in a tangible way by our sponsorship of formal education programmes which may often relate more to a future role than to an individual's current responsibilities.

Mechanisms for career development

In common with our peer companies we have seen deteriorating trends in employee perception levels relative to career opportunities in recent years.

Our response to this has been to concentrate on defining the new scenario through communication and education in order to re-position the career development issue. We have put in place a company-wide information system to publicize available job opportunities. We have studied ways to encourage more lateral movement. Later this year we plan to redefine our remuneration guidelines for lateral assignments to allow greater recognition for career broadening moves.

We have also built on the professional career ladder experience of our technical and sales functions and extended these to other key groups, e.g. finance and customer service.

Other areas of attention include the 'Job Swap' idea where two individuals are encouraged to exchange roles for a defined period of time often in a different function or location.

Management Ideas

These mechanisms have been successful in stabilizing employee satisfaction in this area and we believe, over time, will lead to higher levels of employee satisfaction.

Roles in career development

As indicated earlier in the summary there is now much more emphasis on the role of the individual in career development at 3M. Individuals are seen as the *owners* of their own career development plan and *accountable* for any defined action.

The manager is positioned as the coach in a supporting role, able to provide visibility and recognition and to remove barriers to progress. This contrasts sharply with the more traditional view of the manager's role, i.e. responsible for 'making it all happen'.

The company or organization's role is defined as the provider of appropriate structures, information and processes and the most conducive environment for personal growth. In addition, the company is responsible for *intervening* when and if succession planning for key positions is judged to be fragile or inadequate.

The fine balance between these ideas is a key factor in our overall career development strategy.

Mobility in career development

The final issue in this summary of key influencing factors in career development relates to employee mobility. However effective may be the formal training and development activities in an organization, it is clear to us at 3M that most individual development takes place in and around the job.

We are a global organization operating through more than 50 business divisions, in fifty-eight countries, making 66 000 products with twenty functional centres of expertise. The scope for personal development and growth in such an enterprise is virtually limitless. One possible limiting factor could be restricted employee mobility. We have worked hard to minimize this potential barrier to personal development by putting in place relocation policies at local, European and global levels. Relocation is an expensive business with many associated problems. Some companies have given up on the relocation front seeing it as too complex, too disruptive and too costly.

At 3M we have continued to provide a series of alternative relocation programmes that enable any individual with the right skills, motivation and capability to work in any 3M organization world-wide. Several hundred 3M employees are on the move at any one time to new positions in their own countries or around the globe. Of course this is not for everyone and most people in our company will spend their entire careers at one location or within their own country. The key issue for us is that we have the scope and flexibility for these career development options. The benefits far outweigh the costs. The assignment process acts as an accelerator for management development. A simple analysis of the background and expertise of the company's top 100 managers provides a solid testimony to the effectiveness of this strategy.

Summary

In summary, we see some clear trends that are impacting our organization today and that different individual strategies are required to maximize the likelihood of achieving sustained personal growth and the full realization of potential. At 3M we have found that specific organizational initiatives have worked well in influencing employee perceptions and that the shift in focus to individual ownership for career development is a key factor. We value the acquisition of broad experience through lateral assignments and see the need to provide more recognition for these moves. Finally, we recognize the strength of our diversity as a catalyst for personal growth and the importance of providing the appropriate employee mobility policies to maximize the impact of our diversity or career development.

Source: Conference paper presented by Paul M. Davies, human resources development manager, 3M United Kingdom plc, at the conference 'Managing the Horizontal Organization' organized by the Economist Conferences in London, March 1995.

In flatter organizations and in organizations where teams and teamwork exist, the issue of individual aspirations and career development have become important considerations. The question of individual performance appraisal is partly answered by the introduction of the 360° feedback system but the question of individual career development and rewarding individuals within the team environment still needs to be thought out very carefully.

Putting people together in a team does not mean they will work together as a team. Getting people to work effectively in teams is difficult and has to be managed properly.

Twenty-one questions organizations must ask in forming teams

1. Why do you want to form teams?
2. What type of teams do you want to form?
3. Do you have adequate and appropriate resources to staff the teams?
4. Have you formulated smart, meaningful and attainable objectives?
5. Have you established the time-scale for the task or process objectives?
6. Do these objectives stretch the capabilities of team members?
7. Do the team members understand why they have been formed into teams and have you clarified their roles?
8. What type of training are you going to design and deliver for team members?
9. Do your training programmes cover technical, personal and inter-personal dimensions of team-work?
10. How much time are you going to allow for teams to form, storm, norm and perform?
11. How are you going to promote team maintenance?
12. What should be communicated within the team, to whom, by what method, when and how?
13. What kind of direction are you going to provide to the teams?
14. Have you appointed a coach or a facilitator or a team leader?
15. What actions are you going to have in place to avoid the formation of 'group-think'?
16. Have you designed performance measures for the teams?
17. Are the performance indicators and measures appropriate to team-work and team objectives?
18. How are you going to update the capabilities of team members?
19. Have you given consideration to career development of individuals?
20. How are teams and individuals within the team going to be rewarded?
21. How are you going to introduce changes to the teams?

Having answered all the questions one can then proceed to forming teams. It is also important regularly to monitor the teaming process.

Are you a good team player?

1.	I am a competent and caring person.	Agree/Disagree
2.	I like to communicate my ideas freely.	Agree/Disagree
3.	I seldom question the usefulness of our decisions.	Agree/Disagree
4.	I go along with what others say in order to avoid arguments.	Agree/Disagree
5.	I do not like to say what I really think.	Agree/Disagree
6.	I do trust my manager.	Agree/Disagree
7.	I do not trust all the members of the team.	Agree/Disagree
8.	I like working in the team because I do not like to make decisions.	Agree/Disagree
9.	I do not like to be criticized.	Agree/Disagree
10.	Teams are a nice way of fudging the issues.	Agree/Disagree
11.	I do not like to give my views on the performance of my colleagues.	Agree/Disagree
12.	I do not feel strengthened by my colleagues.	Agree/Disagree
13.	I like to question the way we operate.	Agree/Disagree
14.	I believe tighter supervision produces better results.	Agree/Disagree
15.	Working in teams is a waste of time.	Agree/Disagree
16.	I like to defend my function when I am in a team.	Agree/Disagree
17.	I make an attempt to understand the views of others.	Agree/Disagree
18.	I like to be consulted.	Agree/Disagree
19.	I am not prepared to express my beliefs openly.	Agree/Disagree
20.	I do not like raising delicate issues.	Agree/Disagree
21.	I like thinking up new ideas.	Agree/Disagree
22.	I am ready to face temporary unpopularity if I can improve the situation.	Agree/Disagree
23.	I like talking very much.	Agree/Disagree
24.	I am over-responsive to the team atmosphere.	Agree/Disagree
25.	I have an aptitude for influencing others.	Agree/Disagree
26.	I get very angry and frustrated if I do not get my way.	Agree/Disagree
27.	I like working in groups.	Agree/Disagree
28.	I work better on my own.	Agree/Disagree
29.	I am not good at getting my points across.	Agree/Disagree
30.	I get bored very easily.	Agree/Disagree

Answers: You are a good team member if you agreed to 1, 2, 6, 13, 17, 18, 21, 22, 25 and 27 and disagreed to 3, 4, 5, 7, 8, 9, 10, 11, 12, 14, 15, 16, 19, 20, 23, 24, 26, 28, 29 and 30.

Selected reading

William Bridges (1994) The End of the Job. *Fortune*, September 19.

Brian Domain (1994) The Trouble with Teams. *Fortune*, September 5.

Geert Hofstede (1991) *Cultures and Organizations*. McGraw-Hill.

Ralph L. Kliem and Irwin S. Ludin (1992) *The People Side of Project Management*. Gower.

Christopher Meyer (1994) How the Right Measures Help Teams Excel. *Harvard Business Review*, May-June.

Fons Trompenaars (1993) *Riding the Waves of Culture*. Nicholas Brealey.

11

The knowledge era: computers and communication systems

in brief. "In a time of drastic change it is learners who inherit the future. The learned find themselves equipped to live in a world that no longer exists."
Eric Hoffer

Summary

■ Use of computers – from data processing to information management.
■ Use of computers in business.
■ Computers and organizational transformation.
■ Computers and Porter's competitive forces.

Management Ideas

- Some businesses use computers wrongly.
- Creation of the information society: initiatives in the USA, Japan and Europe.
- Enter the knowledge era: the organization of the twenty-first century.

Knowledge is information + intelligence

From being the learning organization and working with empowered multi-functional teams, organizations now believe that their strategic and competitive advantage lies in the leverage of knowledge. Computers and communication systems have played a key role in enabling organizations to transform themselves into knowledge-based organizations.

Computers and communication systems

In the 1950s and 1960s computers were used to process data and to focus on financial and administrative tasks. Computers enabled companies to gather and store data and convert data into information.

Gradually the computer's impact grew with its scope of application and the depth of its capability. SABRE, the American Airlines travel agency reservation system, began as an internal reservation system in the 1950s. In the mid-1970s it was linked to travel agents. Computers became the most effective competitive weapon in the airline industry. The SABRE system enabled American Airlines to build up a detailed database of people's travel habits, their destinations, how they travelled, and so on.

Computers in business

There are numerous examples to show how businesses are using computers to improve communication with their customers and suppliers and innovate their products.

- American Hospital Supply's ASAP order-entry and inventory control system generated huge sales increases for medical products.
- Computer-aided design (CAD) and computer-aided manufacturing (CAM) became very prominent in the 1980s.
- British Telecom after privatization achieved significant benefits and improved its efficiency by adopting an executive information system (EIS). The software takes raw data and presents it in a very user-friendly form.
- Some companies have reduced their order lead time by as much as 90 per cent by computerizing their operations.
- Some have given their distributors electronic access to their inventory files in order to improve and overcome scheduling problems.
- Many hospitals send pricing and other information to their purchasing agents via a computerized system.
- 'Hole in the wall' automated teller machines (ATMs) were introduced to provide better service and cut the costs of processing cheques and other transactions.
- In retailing, computers are used to inform retailers what they are selling and in what quantities. They can get information on how much they are selling of each product line, who their customers are, and so on.
- In the 1970s supermarkets installed EPOS (electronic point-of-sale) systems. EPOS records each sale using a laser scanner which reads the bar code on the product.
- The story of the success of Wal-Mart is the story of how this business used computers creatively. Wal-Mart set up computer links between each store and the distribution warehouses through electronic data interchange (EDI); it also hooked up to the computers of the firm's main suppliers.
- Wal-Mart also uses computer modelling incorporating over 2500 variables to customize its assortments for particular stores.

Management Ideas

- Many businesses are now controlling their supply chains via computer networks.
- Mrs Fields Cookies relied on its retail operations intelligence system to build a nation-wide chain of 400 outlets without headquarters bureaucracy.
- Otis, the elevator company, installed the OTISLINE computer system to improve the service offered to its customers. According to the consultancy Index Group, OTISLINE revolutionized customer service and it also gained 6 per cent of additional market share.
- Many businesses are linked by computers to carry out functions such as order processing and payments and reducing scheduling problems and inventory overheads.

Today businesses are driven by three success factors – quality, time and cost. Computers have become an enabling technology and many companies are using the computer as a strategic tool to improve overall management and market performance.

Ask not what computers can do for us, but what we can do with computers

- Enabled businesses to process information and its functions, ranging from data management to transactions processing.
- Converted information into knowledge and enabled knowledge-sharing among companies.
- Helped integrating various businesses and managed complex operations.
- Changed 'the way we do business' attitudes and promoted 'out-of-the-box' thinking.
- Questioned the fundamental assumptions of business.
- Opened up various strategic options.
- Made relationship marketing and database marketing possible and effective.
- Enhanced core competencies of businesses.
- Underpinned various change initiatives.
- Enabled teleworking.

The list is not exhaustive. Every day one reads about a new application. The arrival of cheaper computer systems has also provided opportunities for small companies to configure their businesses and use information to compete effectively. Experts are predicting that within the next few years, sales of PCs will break through the 100 million level, thus exceeding annual sales of television sets for the first time.

Each new microprocessor generation brings more power and businesses are not slow in seizing opportunities to explore and exploit greater use of value added communication services in order to enhance business communications and improve competitive positioning.

Computer and competitive forces – some comments

The use of computers has had a significant impact on all competitive forces with the result that companies have to be constantly on their toes to survive in the competitive arena.

Porter's competitive forces

(1)   Barriers to entry

■ Information technology in the form of computers and telecommunications continues to penetrate and transform every aspect of business.
■ Barriers to entry are constantly being eroded due to the development of electronic highways.
■ Information technology has made the economies of scale arguments redundant.

(2) and (3) Bargaining power – suppliers and buyers

■ Computer technology used creatively can help companies to capture, satisfy and retain customers.
■ Companies consider their suppliers as 'partners' and give them access to their inventory files.

Management Ideas

■ Customers have electronic access to pricing and other information in relation to certain products and companies.
■ Computer technology has enabled companies to link with suppliers and customers globally.

(4)   Substitutes

■ Customers can now book flights on almost any airline due to computerized reservation systems.
■ The microcomputer revolution has enabled new products to come to the market in a very short period.
■ The significant advances of computers have created a wide spectrum of new strategic options.
■ Computer technology has accelerated product and process innovation.

Computers that listen and talk are beginning to dominate businesses. There are graphical user interfaces driven by the use of icons and the mouse, notepad computers that can be written on with a pen, and so on. The 'interface revolution' has given many the taste of user-friendly screens.

Companies' mechanisms of control and management as well as communication are changing immensely as we pass into the era of the Internet, information superhighways and computer software. Employees are becoming skilled with their workstations and move between systems without extensive training. Computers are becoming as familiar a part of the business environment as telephones.

Why do some businesses lag behind in computer technology?

■ Computer technology changes entrenched attitudes to 'the way we do business'. There is, therefore, resistance to embracing computer technology wholeheartedly.
■ Some use computers as a window-dressing exercise in order to impress their boards of directors.
■ Some do not understand the capabilities of computer technology.

- Some companies have failed because of complete misunderstanding of users' needs.
- In some cases system development and implementation have proved very costly.

Computer technology and business transformation: beware!

- The misuse of technology can reinforce old habits and block re-engineering by reinforcing old ways of thinking.
- A company that cannot change the way it thinks about IT cannot re-engineer.
- Computer technology should be used innovatively and creatively.
- Computer technology cannot offer solutions if businesses are not capable of identifying problems.

Computers, communication systems and national initiatives

The information society

The USA, Japan and Europe independently but in close concert during 1993 and 1994 launched separate information society programmes. According to G. Russell Pipe, of the Global Information Infrastructure Commission, based in the USA, the shared information infrastructure objectives of these initiatives can be summarized as follows:

- 'exploring opportunities offered by advanced computer and communications technologies, new products and services;
- improving quality of life by offering new working life styles; greater personal interaction, reducing environmental problems caused by energy overuse;
- raising efficiency and productivity, stimulating economic growth and trade competitiveness;

Management Ideas

■ modernizing all aspects of society;
■ addressing environmental problems by more efficient use of resources and energy.'

The main objectives for the USA, Japan and Europe for constructing national information infrastructures (NII) are as highlighted below:

The USA

Network of communication networks; computers, databases linking homes, businesses, schools and libraries to a vast array of electronic information resources and creating commercial opportunities.

The NII task force has been set up to work on ways to materialize these objectives.

Japan

Fibre optic information communication networks to every business and household for an intellectually creative society able to meet social and economic restructuring in the twenty-first century.

Japan is advocating a 'shift of perspective in which the goods- and energy-oriented twentieth century gives way to the information- and knowledge-oriented twenty-first century based on info-communications infrastructure.' According to the Telecommunications Council of the Ministry of Posts and Telecommunications, 'In the intellectually creative society based on high performance info-communications of the twenty-first century, great importance will be attached to the free creation, circulation and sharing of information and knowledge as social and economic assets.'

Europe

Creation of an information society based on trans-European networks and liberal telecommunications markets to create jobs and strengthen competitiveness.

An action plan for planning 'Europe's Way to the Information Society' was presented to the European heads of state meeting in Corfu, Greece in June 1994. The plan was designed by a high level working group chaired by EU Commissioner Martin Bangemann. The core principles of the EU action plan are to:

- Strengthen industrial competitiveness.
- Create new jobs.
- Promote new forms of work organization.
- Improve quality of life and the environment.
- Respond to social need.
- Raise efficiency and cost-effectiveness of public services.

In February 1995, a G7 ministerial conference took place in Brussels. The conference served two purposes:

1. To confirm that the leading industrialized nations are committed to national information infrastructure programmes leading to information societies.
2. To provide actual demonstrations of a whole array of applications.

In preparation for the ministerial conference, a group of business leaders headed by Mr Carlo Benedetti, President of Olivetti, prepared a draft policy paper entitled Building a Global Information Society – A Call for Government Action.

A similar request was also heard at the Asia-Pacific Economic Co-operation (APEC) ministerial meeting held in Seoul in May 1995.

There is no looking back – enter the knowledge era

The successful corporations of the next millennium will be those who are knowledge-driven with world-wide information highways, massive computer power and leadership styles that will facilitate value-added by all employees.

The twenty-first century is going to be dominated by knowledge-driven companies. Stan Davies, author of *Future Perfect* (1987), has predicted that all businesses, high tech as well low tech, face the choice of launching new products and services that are knowledge based.

Knowledge is rapidly becoming the most important resource of the future. Davies's latest book, *The Monster Under the Bed*, co-authored with Jim Botkin, declares:

> 'Today knowledge is often a businessmen's most valuable commodity and knowledge workers are often its most valuable resource. Knowledge is an increasing portion of the value of an offering in the marketplace and the basis for competitive advantage.'

It is said that in business, information is knowledge and 'knowledge is power' (*The Economist*). Louis Gerstner, chairman of IBM said, 'Powerful networks will increasingly unlock corporate knowledge and move it to people who can use it effectively and creatively.'

The concept of knowledge is not a new one. The first learning organization to realize the importance of knowledge was IBM which adopted the word 'Think' as its motto. What subsequently happened to IBM was that thinking was not capitalized into action to respond to the rapidly changing market environment.

The learning organizations of the 1990s will take advantage of convergence of technologies and become the networked knowledge organizations of the twenty-first century. Suppliers, partners and customers will be linked by computer technology to share skills, costs and access to one another's markets. Some say that come the twenty-first century, the marketplace will be replaced by cyberplace.

What of those who lag behind or are not prepared? They should ponder upon the moral of the following story:

> Once upon a time there were two businessmen walking in a jungle. Suddenly, they heard the roar of an angry and hungry tiger. One businessman opened up his rucksack and took his running shoes out. As he was putting them on the other businessman remarked, 'You are crazy; you cannot outrun the tiger!' The other businessman replied, 'No, you are right. I cannot outrun the tiger but I can outrun you.'

And the moral of the story? Be prepared to outrun your competitors.

The last word on the role of knowledge must go to Peter Drucker. According to Drucker:

> But the modern organization is a destabilizer. It must be organized for innovation. . . And it must be organized for the systematic abandonment of whatever is established, customary, familiar and comfortable. . . In short, it must be organized for constant change. The organization's function is to put knowledge to work – on tools, products and processes; on the design of work; on knowledge itself. It is the nature of knowledge that it changes fast and that today's certainties always become tomorrow's absurdities.

He goes on to write:

> For managers, the dynamics of knowledge impose one clear imperative: every organization has to build the management of change into its very structure.
>
> (Peter Drucker: *Managing in a Time of Great Change* (1995). Butterworth–Heinemann.)

Selected reading

Stan Davies and Jim Botkin (1994) *The Monster Under the Bed*. Simon & Schuster.
Peter Drucker (1995) *Managing in a Time of Great Change*. Butterworth–Heinemann.
The Economist (1995) A Survey of Retailing. March 4.
The EIU Report (1991) *Executive Information Systems*.
The American Management Association Magazine (1995) *Management Review*. Technological Transformation of Enterprises. Nov.

Epilogue:
Memo from all employees to the chief executive officers

To: Chief executive officers
From: All employees
Subject: Is there anyone out there listening?

You have indicated to us the necessity for business to improve product and quality service, to benchmark in order to adopt best practice, to re-engineer processes and businesses and to become customer-service minded. 'People are our greatest asset' you say in our annual company report. You ask us to give you full support and commitment and to understand the nature of the changes undertaken by the company.

You have our full support. You have to make special efforts to promote understanding of the various change efforts but do please make sure that we do not become 'initiative fatigued'. We would like to draw your attention to the following:

Organizational schizophrenia

In our company annual report to shareholders and to us there are numerous platitudes about us. 'People are our greatest asset', 'People are our life and blood', 'It's our people who make things happen'. And yet when there is a hint of crisis and you are put under pressure from your board and shareholders to reduce costs the first thing you do is 'downsize' the organization. Downsizing is simply getting rid

Memo from all employees

of people without analysing the loss of capabilities. Getting rid of people is the easiest and the 'macho' thing to do in order to buy time or impress the board. The true character of the inspirational leader in our view is facing crisis with courage and imagination. You only get rid of people as a very last resort when everything else has failed. In a crisis situation you need to analyse the capabilities that exist within the organization and make use of them to perform strategic manoeuvres.

If you find that you have 'surplus' people in your company, why not redeploy them to acquire new skills so that you do not lose their experience and loyalty? Of course, in the short term you will still have high costs and you will not be able to impress your board and shareholders but in the medium and long term if you face the crisis with courage and imagination we will give our full support and the company will come through the crisis and sustain the survival instinct for a very long time to come. You will gain respect and trust from us. This is one of the ways you can win trust.

If you have to make some of us redundant as a last resort please do treat us as human beings with feelings. When you did make a hundred of our colleagues redundant last time, some of them were on holiday and some of them were asked to leave the office within a day. Our manager was asked to clear his desk within ten minutes and return the company car key immediately. There are many horror stories of the way this company has treated people when getting rid of them.

With waves of redundancies we also find it difficult to concentrate on our work and trust your leadership. We constantly ask 'who next?' Not a very nice feeling!

What can we do for the company?

We are one of the groups of stakeholders of the business and we want the business to succeed just as you and your board do. We require leaders we can trust and who trust us. Trust has to be institutionalized and made transparent so that we feel it in our hearts and minds.

Tell us openly about our company strategy and objectives. Give us the chance to help out during crisis.

Management Ideas

Do not respond to every management fad but when you do, consider implications throughout the entire business. We have read that change initiatives such as re-engineering lead to 'corporate anorexia' and 70 per cent of re-engineering initiatives fail because they have not been done properly.

We are willing to change our 'jobs' and adopt different roles within the company. Give us adequate and appropriate training to become a multi-skilled workforce so that we can help the company be responsive to changing customer needs.

Empowerment

We work in teams now and we are told we are empowered. To perform key roles within the teams the human resources department has arranged for us to attend an Outward Bound course and attend team-building seminars. We have enjoyed the course and had a very pleasurable time together. But there is no one able to help us transfer the experience to the workplace. We need help to solve problems and make decisions. We believe we should be consulted on our training needs. Training should not be left to the human resources department.

Career development

We understand there are not going to be promotions in a traditional sense. We are responsible for our own career development. There is information available in our library about various courses available. We do, however, need career counselling within the company.

Our company has various schemes to promote horizontal mobility. We are seconded to other departments if we wish to acquire broad experience. This is very good idea as it gives us a chance to understand how different businesses work.

One thing, however, has not been addressed sufficiently. As we take care of our destiny as the organization structure is becoming flat, the payment and incentive system has not

Memo from all employees

changed very much. We believe the incentive and pay scheme should be consistent with the changes taking place.

We also believe that a new psychological contract is developing between the employees and the top management. For such a contract to be effective you have to promise us support and give us the opportunity to acquire new skills. Employability rather than stability should be the centrepiece of this contract.

We promise to give you our full support and commitment. But you have to demonstrate the courage of your convictions in us, your people. Open communication, trust and credibility should be the key attributes of inspirational chief executive officers.

Index

Index

Index

Index

Index